The Easy Way to
WILD
FLOWER
Recognition

John Kilbracken

GUILD PUBLISHING
LONDON

The author wishes to thank Dr Bob Press of
the Natural History Museum and Dr Tom Cope
of the Royal Botanic Gardens for their help
in the preparation of this book.

This edition published 1985 by
Book Club Associates
By arrangement with Kingfisher Books Limited

Illustrations by Wendy Bramall and Shirley Willis
Phototypeset by Southern Positives and Negatives (SPAN)
Lingfield, Surrey
Colour separations by Newsele Litho Ltd, Milan, London
Printed in Italy by Vallardi Industrie Grafiche, Milan

How to Use this Book

This book has been written with only one end in view – to help the beginner to identify, more easily than ever before, the wild flowers most likely to be seen in Britain and Ireland. It does this in a way that is quite different from all the other flower identification books available. With the other books, unless you know the family to which the flower you have seen belongs, you must go through the whole volume looking at the illustrations and reading often complex descriptions until you decide which is the right one.

In *The Easy Way to Wild Flower Recognition*, you are led through the book by a number of simple questions about the flower you are identifying, till you quickly arrive at the answer. It is a companion volume to my two earlier books, *The Easy Way to Bird Recognition* and *The Easy Way to Tree Recognition*, which used precisely the same technique for identifying birds and trees.

If you glance at the text, you will see that it consists of a series of Questions and Answers, numbered consecutively from 1 to 373. The Questions are numbered in blue, the Answers in yellow. When you wish to identify a flower, always start at Question 1. Have a look at it now: it asks you what colour the flower is. You should have little trouble in deciding on the correct reply, which directs you to the next Question. So you are led on, rather as though you were following the clues in a treasure hunt, towards identification. The Questions are extremely simply worded, and there is nearly always a passage of text and illustrations to help you choose your answer. All technical terms you might not know or understand have been avoided; or, if this sometimes proved impossible, they are carefully explained.

After perhaps as few as three Questions, and never more than a dozen, you'll find that you arrive at an Answer. Here the flower is illustrated in colour, with a passage of descriptive text giving details that will help in identification. The months when the flower is most likely to be in bloom are also given. In almost every case, each species has an Answer to itself, and your trail is at an end. Occasionally, where two species are very similar, they are taken together in the same Answer. Both species are illustrated, so you should have no trouble deciding between them.

Now let's see how the book works in practice, taking the daisy – a flower almost everyone knows already – as an example. Turn to Question 1: 'What colour are its flowers?' The daisy's petals are tipped with red and it has a yellow centre, but the text tells you clearly: 'If two or more colours are present, choose the one that is most noticeable.' There is no doubt, in the case of the daisy, that this is WHITE, and you are therefore directed at once to Question 87. This asks whether or not the plant grows in water. Since it does not, go on to 93. This asks you about the leaves – whether they are alternate, opposite, whorled or basal. If you don't know precisely what these words mean when applied to leaves, they are carefully explained in simple language, and illustrated, so you should see at once that the daisy's leaves are BASAL (meaning that they all grow at the base of the plant). You are then directed to 171.

The flowers grow SINGLY, which leads you to 172; they are REGULAR, which takes you to 173; and each flower has MORE THAN SIX PETALS, which brings you on to 182. This, after a 'treasure-trail' of only six Questions, is your Answer. A read of the text and a look at the illustration should leave you in no doubt that you have identified the flower correctly.

If you happen to arrive at an Answer that is clearly incorrect, there are only two possible explanations. Either you have made a mistake somewhere along the line, and should go back to the beginning and try again, or you have come across a flower not common enough to be included in the book. It would have been impossible to include all those you might come across, so I decided to limit the number to the 200 commonest species. This was not an easy task. It may sometimes happen that a flower found quite often in your particular neighbourhood, or in a stretch of the country you visit, is not among them. In such cases you should consult a more comprehensive guide. But the chosen species should cover all those beginners are most likely to see in their first year or two, unless they are specially lucky.

In some ways, this book should be far easier to use than its predecessors on trees and birds. Flowers are much more distinctive than leaves – on which I mainly relied in the tree book – and they vary very little in colour, size and shape. Exceptions to this rule, like the flowers of the comfrey, which may be white, bluish-purple or pink, have been taken into account, and you will arrive at comfrey whether you choose white, red or blue as your answer to Question 1, though by completely different routes. Unlike a bird, a plant stays put and you have all the time in the world to examine it closely, to take measurements if necessary, and to check all minor details.

I should like to recommend that you slip this book in your pocket and take it with you when you are out looking for flowers, rather than picking the flowers and bringing them back to identify at home. In the case of certain rare species, it is against the law to do so. It is always against the law to *dig up* wild flowers, roots and all, without the permission of the landowner. But as a general rule, you should not pick wild flowers unless they are of a species seen plentifully in the neighbourhood. Also, by taking the book to the flower, you ensure that the flower is fresh and therefore easier to identify, and that you have the whole plant available for inspection.

I have not included a glossary in the book because the few difficult words that are used (e.g. involucre, bract) are always explained when they occur. But one important point should be made in this connection. Some flowers – almost all daisy-like or dandelion-like – appear to have one or more rings of radiating petals. In fact these are *not* petals. Each of them is technically an individual flower known as a *ray floret*. However, in this book I treat them as petals, which they appear to be to a beginner. Any reference to petals should therefore be taken as including ray florets.

JK
Killegar
1984

1   What colour are its flowers?

In most cases the answer will be self-evident. If two or more colours are present, choose the one that is most noticeable.

It is only with purplish flowers that you may feel any doubt. Make it the rule to choose 'Red or reddish' if they are pink, purple-red, or any other colour that seems on balance closer to red than blue. Choose 'Blue or bluish' if they are violet, lilac, purple-blue, or any other colour that seems closer to blue than red.

Yellow [2]
White or greenish-white [87]
Red or reddish [192]
Blue or bluish [292]
Green or brown [342]

2   Is the plant growing in water?

(from 1)
Answer 'Yes' if the lower part of the stem, or all the stem, is submerged in water. Answer 'No' if the plant is growing on dry land, or if only the roots are submerged.

Yes [3]   No [6]

3   Are the flowers regular?

(from 2)
Answer 'Yes' if all the petals of each flower are equal in size and the same shape. Otherwise answer 'No'.

Yes [4]   No [5]

Irregular

Regular

4   YELLOW WATER-LILY
(Nuphar lutea)

(from 3)

This water-lily always grows in still or slow-moving water. Its solitary flowers (4–6cm) have 5 petals and grow from stalks that usually rise a few inches above the water; but the large, glossy, heart-shaped leaves float flatly on the surface. Flowers June–August.

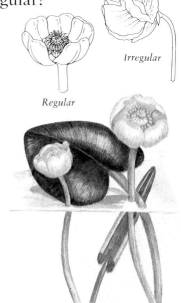

(from 3)

GREATER BLADDERWORT
(Utricularia vulgaris)

This rootless plant grows only in still water. Its flowers (12–15mm) grow alternately along the upper part of its erect stem, which also bears a few very small leaves, stalkless and alternate. Flowers July–September.

 # How do the leaves grow?

(from 2)

Leaves are described as being alternate, opposite, whorled or basal, depending on how they grow along their stem or stalk.

Alternate leaves grow singly, on alternating sides of it. Opposite leaves are in pairs, and whorled leaves in groups of 3 or more around it. Choose 'Basal only' if all the leaves grow at the very base of the plant. Choose 'None visible' if no leaves are present when the flower is in bloom.

The drawings should make your choice quite easy.

Alternate   7

Opposite or whorled   59

Basal only   73

None visible   86

Greater bladderwort

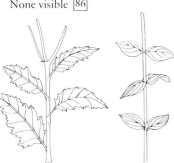

Alternate   *Opposite*   *Whorled*   *Basal only*

7   Do the flowers lack petals?

(from 6)

This question needs no elaboration.   Yes ☐ 8   No ☐ 15

8   Are the flowers very small?

(from 7)

Answer 'Yes' if the flowers are no more than 4mm in diameter.   Otherwise answer 'No'.

Yes ☐ 9   No ☐ 12

9   Is the plant aromatic?

(from 8)

Answer 'Yes' if the leaves give off a pleasant aroma when crushed. Otherwise answer 'No'.

Yes ☐ 10   No ☐ 11

10   MUGWORT
(Artemisia vulgaris)

(from 9)

The flowers are brownish yellow, bell-shaped and very small (3–4mm), growing in loose clusters at the end of the branching stems. The plant grows erect and may exceed 100cm in height. The stalkless leaves are deeply divided and clasp the stem. Mugwort is often found on dry wasteland and by roadsides. It flowers July–September.

COMMON GROUNDSEL
(Senecio vulgaris)

(from 9)

The undistinguished groundsel is a weed of wasteland and arable ground. Its very small flowers grow in loose clusters. The leaves are deeply lobed and are stalkless, grasping the stem, except at the base of the plant. Seldom exceeds 25cm in height. Flowers almost all year.

 ## Are the flowers flat-topped?

(from 8)

Answer 'Yes' if the flowers (7–12mm) are flat-topped. Answer 'No' if they are rather smaller, and domed or rounded in shape.

Yes 13   No 14

Flat-topped flowers   *Rounded flowers*

 TANSY
(Tanacetum vulgare)

(from 12)

Tansy is distinguished by its button-like flowers, which have no radiating petals or florets. They grow in quite dense, flat-topped clusters, 7–15cm in diameter. The leaves are so deeply divided that they are almost fern-like; they are hairless and stalkless. Tansy grows on wasteland, by hedgerows or at roadsides. Flowers July–September.

14 **PINEAPPLEWEED**
(Matricaria matricarioides)
(from 12)

The flowers of pineappleweed
(6–10mm) grow in small clusters on
quite long individual stalks. The
compound leaves are extremely
deeply divided, so that they are
almost fern-like. The plant grows
erect and has a vague smell of
pineapple if crushed. Usually found
on pathways, tracks, or other
trampled ground. Flowers June–
July.

15 Are the flowers very
large and showy?
(from 7)

Answer 'Yes' if the flowers are iris-
like and very large (8–10cm), with
1–3 blooms on each flattened, erect
stem. Otherwise answer 'No'.

Yes [16]

No [17]

Iris-like flower

16 **YELLOW IRIS**
(Iris pseudacorus)
(from 15)

This tall, handsome plant is quite
unmistakable. It reaches a height of
150cm and has large flowers up to
10cm in diameter. Their three larger
petals alternate with three smaller
ones. The very long, narrow leaves
have conspicuous parallel veins.
Yellow iris grows in moist or wet
ground, often beside a river, and
likes land that is flooded in winter.
Flowers May–July.

17   Are the flowers regular?

(from 15)

Answer 'Yes' if all the petals of each flower are equal in size and the same shape; or, if there are two or more rings of petals in each flower, the petals in each ring are equal and the same shape. Otherwise answer 'No'.

Yes 18   No 51

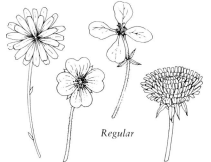
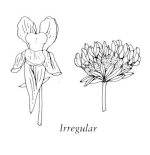

Regular   *Irregular*

18   How many petals has each flower?

(from 17)

Count the number of petals in each flower and choose your answer accordingly.

4 19
5 27
6–12 42
Over 12 43

19   Are the leaves composite?

(from 18)

Answer 'Yes' if each leaf is composed of several separate leaflets. Answer 'No' if the leaves, though they may be deeply divided, are each single and independent.

Yes 20   No 23

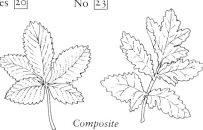

Not composite

Composite

What size are the flowers?

(from 19)

Measure the diameter of an average-sized flower to decide which is the right answer.

2–2½cm 21
Up to 1½cm 22
Over 2½cm 117

21 GREATER CELANDINE
(Chelidonium majus)

(from 20)

This is a member of the poppy family and is no relation to the well-known lesser celandine (see 74). It is a leafy plant with roughly toothed, almost hairless foliage. Its quite large flowers (about 2cm) are in clusters of 4–6. Often grows on walls, or on the banks of hedgerows. Flowers May–August.

Greater celandine

22 TORMENTIL
(Potentilla erecta)

(from 20)

Tormentil usually grows more or less erect. It prefers acid soils and is found on fens and bogland as well as in fields. Its petals are roughly heart-shaped and only slightly longer than the narrow sepals between them. The leaves at the base of the plant have three leaflets and are stalked, whilst the upper leaves are stalkless and have 3–5 leaflets. Flowers June–September.

Tormentil

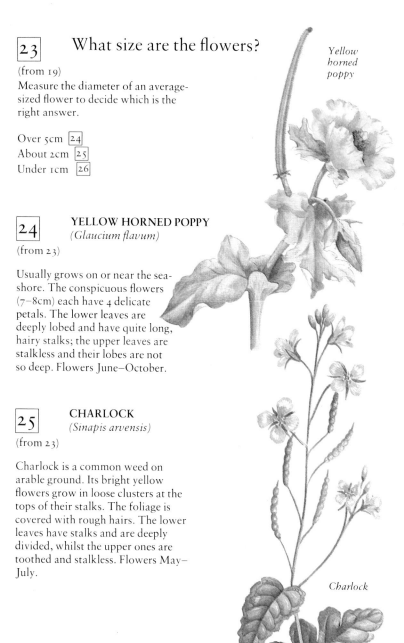

23   What size are the flowers?

Yellow horned poppy

(from 19)

Measure the diameter of an average-sized flower to decide which is the right answer.

Over 5cm   24
About 2cm   25
Under 1cm   26

24   YELLOW HORNED POPPY
(Glaucium flavum)

(from 23)

Usually grows on or near the sea-shore. The conspicuous flowers (7–8cm) each have 4 delicate petals. The lower leaves are deeply lobed and have quite long, hairy stalks; the upper leaves are stalkless and their lobes are not so deep. Flowers June–October.

25   CHARLOCK
(Sinapis arvensis)

(from 23)

Charlock is a common weed on arable ground. Its bright yellow flowers grow in loose clusters at the tops of their stalks. The foliage is covered with rough hairs. The lower leaves have stalks and are deeply divided, whilst the upper ones are toothed and stalkless. Flowers May–July.

Charlock

This is a common plant on wasteland
and is also found by roadsides or
hedgerows or on arable land. Its very
small flowers grow in quite long
clusters. The lower leaves are deeply
lobed with the largest lobe at the end;
the upper leaves are more variable.
The erect stem may reach a height of
almost 100cm and has branching
flower-stalks. Flowers May–September.

27   Are the leaves composite?

(from 18)

Answer 'Yes' if each leaf is composed
of several separate leaflets. Answer
'No' if the leaves, though they may
be deeply divided, are each single and
independent.

Yes | 28 | No | 31 |

Composite

Not composite

28   Do the flowers grow singly?

(from 27)

Answer 'Yes' if each flower is
solitary, with its own stalk to itself.
Answer 'No' if many flowers grow
close together in a spike at the end of
the stem.

Yes | 29 | No | 30 |

Flowers single   *Flowers in spike*

29 SILVERWEED
(Potentilla anserina)
(from 28)

The leaves of silverweed are covered
with silky hairs, especially the
undersides, making them silver-
white. Each leaf has many toothed
leaflets, alternately quite large and
very small. The plant grows in damp
fields and on roadsides. Its flowers
(10–18mm) have rounded petals.
Never reaches a great height but
sends out rooting runners up to
almost 100cm in length. Flowers
June–August.

30 COMMON AGRIMONY
(Agrimonia eupatoria)
(from 28)

This plant is to be found on
roadsides, at the edge of meadows
and in hedgerows. Its small flowers
(5–8mm) form a regular spike several
centimetres long. The undersides of
the leaves are hairy and greyish. Each
is composed of several quite large,
toothed leaflets, alternating with
smaller ones. Flowers June–August.

31 Is the plant growing in wet ground?
(from 27)

This question needs no elaboration.

Yes 32   No 35

32 Are the leaves heart-shaped?
(from 31)

Answer 'Yes' if the large, glossy
leaves are noticeably heart-shaped.
Otherwise answer 'No'.   Yes 33   No 34

33 MARSH-MARIGOLD
(Caltha palustris)
(from 32)

The conspicuous, glossy flowers of
marsh-marigold or kingcup are large
(3–5cm) and golden yellow. The
toothed leaves are completely
hairless, as is the hollow stem. This
plant almost always grows in or near
water or on very damp ground, often
by a river. Flowers March–July.

Marsh-marigold

Lesser spearwort

34 LESSER SPEARWORT
(Ranunculus flammula)
(from 32)

Lesser spearwort is a member of the
buttercup family, but differs from the
others in having sharply pointed
leaves that are not lobed or divided.

Its flowers, which are 8–20mm in
size, tend to be smaller than those of
other buttercups and are less glossy.
They grow in loose clusters, each
with its own independent stalk.
Found in damp places, often in
ditches or beside water. Flowers
May–September.

35 | Does each flower have a noticeable stalk?

(from 31)

Answer 'Yes' if the flowers grow singly, or in loose clusters of 2–5 independent flowers, each with a definite stalk. Answer 'No' if they are arranged in clusters with many flowers that are stalkless or nearly so.

Yes 36   No 41

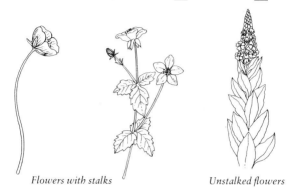

Flowers with stalks   *Unstalked flowers*

36 | Are the flowers a bright, glossy yellow?

(from 35)

Answer 'Yes' if it is a buttercup, with the well-known glossy yellow flowers. Otherwise answer 'No'.

Yes 37   No 38

37 | MEADOW BUTTERCUP
(Ranunculus acris)
(from 36) **CREEPING BUTTERCUP**
(Ranunculus repens)

These are the two commonest buttercups and they are so similar that it is best to consider them together. The main difference is that the flower-stalks of the meadow buttercup are smooth, whilst the creeping buttercup's are noticeably furrowed. The former is usually seen in open fields, whilst the latter is also found in damp ditches or by roadsides.

Creeping buttercup

Both species have conspicuous yellow flowers ($1\frac{1}{2}$–$2\frac{1}{2}$cm), deeply divided leaves and erect stems. (The creeping buttercup gets its name because it puts out many runners, which root at intervals.) Both flower April–September.

Meadow buttercup

38 Is the plant fleshy?

(from 36)

Answer 'Yes' if the stems and leaves are hairless and noticeably fleshy, and the leaves have an unusual swollen shape. Otherwise answer 'No'.

Yes 39   No 40

39 BITING STONECROP
(*Sedum acre*)

(from 38)

The leaves of biting stonecrop, like those of other plants in the same family, are unusual in being plump and fleshy, without veins or stalks. The flowers grow in small clusters of 2–5. The plant is typically found growing on walls, or on dry, stony ground. Flowers June–July.

Biting stonecrop

40 HERB BENNET
(*Geum urbanum*)

(from 38)

Herb bennet, as indicated by its other name, wood avens, is usually found in woods or shady hedgerows. Its flowers (10–18mm) grow in small, loose clusters, each with its own flower stalk. They have 5 prominent sepals, almost as long as the petals and at first visible between them, alternating with 5 shorter ones. Flowers June–August.

Herb bennet

Aaron's rod

41 **AARON'S ROD**
(Verbascum thapsus)
(from 35)

This plant, also known as great mullein, is distinguished by its soft, downy leaves. They are grey-white and mostly stalkless. It grows erect and may exceed 100cm in height, with a long regular spike of tightly-packed flowers. Often found on waste ground or dry roadsides, it flowers from June to August.

42 **GOLDENROD**
(Solidago virgaurea)
(from 18)

The flowers of goldenrod may have 6–12 petals, and are arranged in loose clusters around their stalks. The oval leaves are slightly toothed and almost stalkless. This plant has two quite different habitats: on high ground, where it may grow among mountain rocks to a maximum height of 20cm, and in lowland country, where it is found in hedgerows or woodland and may exceed 100cm. Flowers July–September.

Goldenrod

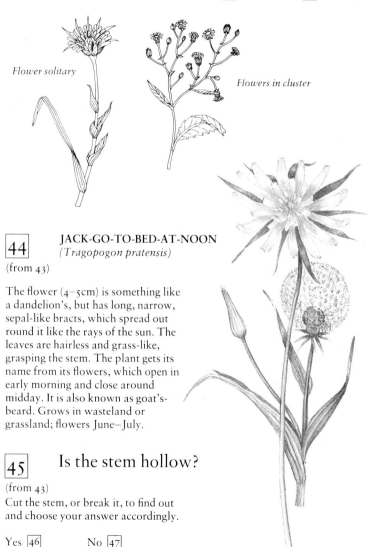

43 Do the flowers grow singly?

(from 18)

Answer 'Yes' if each flower is solitary, with its own stem to itself. Answer 'No' if many flowers grow close together in a spike or cluster at the end of the stem.

Yes 44   No 45

Flower solitary

Flowers in cluster

44 JACK-GO-TO-BED-AT-NOON
(Tragopogon pratensis)

(from 43)

The flower (4–5cm) is something like a dandelion's, but has long, narrow, sepal-like bracts, which spread out round it like the rays of the sun. The leaves are hairless and grass-like, grasping the stem. The plant gets its name from its flowers, which open in early morning and close around midday. It is also known as goat's-beard. Grows in wasteland or grassland; flowers June–July.

45 Is the stem hollow?

(from 43)

Cut the stem, or break it, to find out and choose your answer accordingly.

Yes 46   No 47

SMOOTH SOW-THISTLE
(Sonchus oleraceus)

46 (from 45)

The flowers (2–2½cm) are pale yellow and grow in loose clusters at the end of branching stems. The plant is erect and may exceed 100cm in height. All its leaves have rather spiny teeth; they are stalkless and grasp the stem at their bases. The lower leaves are deeply divided. This is a weed of wasteland, arable ground and roadsides, often growing near walls. Flowers June–August.

47 (from 45)

What shape are the leaves?

A lobe is a deep indentation in the margin of a leaf. You have to decide if the leaves are all without lobes, if those at the base of the plant are quite noticeably lobed, or if all the leaves are so deeply divided that each division almost forms a separate leaflet. The drawings should make it quite easy to decide.

All leaves unlobed 48
Basal leaves lobed 49
All deeply divided 50

Unlobed   *Lobed basal leaves*   *Deeply divided*

HAWKWEED
(Hieracium)

(from 47)

The hawkweeds form a specially difficult group because up to 300 different species have been identified in the British Isles, some of them so similar that it takes an expert to distinguish them. They form a study in themselves and it is not intended to differentiate between them here.

All hawkweeds have flowers like small dandelions, arranged in loose clusters at the ends of usually unbranched stems. They normally have narrow, toothed leaves, which are hairy underneath and may or may not be stalked. The stems, too, are hairy, and give out a bitter, white liquid if cut or broken. Hawkweeds prefer some shade and are often found in open woodland, by roadsides or in hedgerows, but also in grassland. Flowers June–September.

Hawkweed

Nipplewort

Smooth hawk's beard

NIPPLEWORT
(Lapsana communis)
(from 47) **SMOOTH HAWK'S-BEARD**
(Crepis capillaris)

These two plants are quite similar and it is best to take them together. In both cases the flowers (1–2cm) are like small dandelions in loose clusters; and in both the upper leaves are very variable in shape. The most noticeable difference is the shape of the leaves at the base of the plant: those of nipplewort are roughly toothed, with one large lobe and two or more smaller ones, whilst hawk's-beard's are lobed more regularly along most of all of their length. Both grow on wasteland – nipplewort (flowers July–September) prefers shady ground, whilst hawk's-beard (flowers June–September) may grow in open fields.

| 50 |

(from 47)

COMMON RAGWORT
(Senecio jacobaea)

Ragwort is a common weed of neglected grassland, which spreads rapidly and can take over large areas. Its bright yellow flowers ($1\frac{1}{2}$–$2\frac{1}{2}$cm) have up to a dozen radiating florets (which look like petals) and are arranged in quite close clusters at the ends of branching stems. The leaves are deeply divided, mostly stalkless, and hairless or nearly so. Flowers June–October.

Common ragwort

| 51 |

(from 17)

Are the leaves composite?

Answer 'Yes' if each leaf is composed of several separate leaflets. Answer 'No' if the leaves, though they may be deeply divided, are each single and independent.

Yes 52   No 57

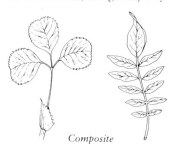

Composite

Not composite

52   Are the flowers woolly?

(from 51)

Answer 'Yes' if the green sepals at
the base of each flower in the cluster
are clothed with woolly white hair.
Otherwise answer 'No'.   Yes 53   No 54

53   KIDNEY VETCH
          (Anthyllis vulneraria)

(from 52)

This plant grows almost erect, with
many closely-packed clusters of
irregular flowers, shaped like those
of a pea. Each flowerhead has its
own stalk, and there is a ring of leaf-
like bracts where it joins the
flowerhead. The leaflets are arranged
in pairs, with the largest one at the
end, then becoming progressively
smaller. Grows in dry grassland,
often by the sea. Flowers June–
August.

54   What size are the flowers?

(from 52)

Measure the diameter of an average-
sized flower and decide on your
answer accordingly.   10–15mm 55
                                   2–3mm 56

55   BIRD'S-FOOT TREFOIL
          (Lotus corniculatus)

(from 54)

Bird's-foot trefoil belongs to the pea
family, and its flowers (1–1½cm long)
have the unusual, irregular shape of
those of other members of the family.
Most of the stem lies prostrate, but
the ends turn upward, bearing loose
clusters of 2–7 bright yellow flowers.
Normally grows in meadows and
pasture. Flowers June–September.

56

BLACK MEDICK
(Medicago lupulina)

(from 54)

Each little flowerhead of black medick appears spherical in shape, but on examination is seen to consist of 10–50 tiny individual flowers (2–3mm). Each leaf is divided into three rounded, toothed leaflets, forming a classic trefoil, and there are two more leaflets at the base of each leaf-stalk. Black medick is a sprawling plant, but may sometimes approach 50mm in height. It is generally downy and produces black fruit. Usually found in grassy, open places. Flowers April–August.

57 Does each flower grow singly?

(from 51)

Answer 'Yes' if each flower grows independently on its own quite long stalk. Choose 'No' if the flowers are almost stalkless, in a tightly-grouped cluster.

Yes 327   No 58

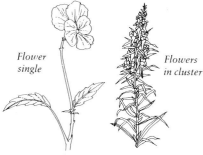

Flower single

Flowers in cluster

58

COMMON TOADFLAX
(Linaria vulgaris)

(from 57 and 71)

The leaves of common toadflax, which are long and narrow, may be alternate, opposite or whorled. The unusual irregular flowers ($1\frac{1}{2}$–$2\frac{1}{2}$cm long) are arranged in a long spike at the end of each flowering stem. The plant grows in grassland or by roadsides. Flowers June–December.

Are the flowers regular?

(from 6)

Answer 'Yes' if all the petals of each flower are equal in size and the same shape. Otherwise answer 'No'.

Yes 60   No 67

Regular   *Irregular*

How many petals has each flower?

(from 59)

Count the number of petals in each flower and choose your answer accordingly.

4 61
5 62

LADY'S BEDSTRAW
(Galium verum)

(from 60)

This distinctive plant has perfectly regular, small flowers (2–4mm), growing in quite loose clusters at the ends of branching stems, which are square and rather hairy. The narrow leaves grow in whorls of 8–12. It thrives in dry, grassy land and in hedgerows or wasteland. Flowers July–August.

62   Is the plant prostrate?

(from 60)

Answer 'Yes' if, for most of its
length, the stem is lying prostrate
along the ground. Answer 'No' if it is
erect.

Yes 63   No 64

Prostrate stem

Erect stem

63   **YELLOW PIMPERNEL**
            (Lysimachia nemorum)

(from 62)

The little yellow flowers rise at
intervals from the prostrate stem,
each on its own stalk. There are
noticeable green sepals alternating
between the petals. The hairless,
toothless leaves are shiny and oval
with very short stalks. This plant
prefers shade and grows in woodland
or hedgerows. Flowers May–July.

64   Are the stems square?

(from 62)

Answer 'Yes' if the stem has four
flanges or wings, so that it appears
square in cross-section. Answer 'No'
if it has only two flanges and they are
less conspicuous.

Yes 65   No 66

Square stem   *Rounded stem*

(from 64)

65 SQUARE-STEMMED ST JOHN'S-WORT
(Hypericum tetrapterum)

Square-stemmed St John's-wort differs from its near relative perforate St John's-wort (see 66) mainly because of its square stem and smaller flowers (1cm). These grow in a loose cluster at the end of their stem. The plant rises erect and is hairless; it prefers damp ground and often grows near water. Flowers June–September.

Perforate St John's-wort

Square-stemmed St John's-wort

66 PERFORATE ST JOHN'S-WORT
(Hypericum perforatum)

(from 64)

In every way similar to square-stemmed St John's-wort (see 65), except for its larger flowers (2cm) and more rounded stalk.

67 Is the stem square?

(from 59)

You will have no difficulty deciding whether the stem is square, with four straight sides, instead of being rounded as is usual. Choose your answer accordingly.

Yes 68
No 69

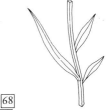

Square stem

68 MEADOW VETCHLING
(Lathyrus pratensis)

(from 67)

The bright yellow, pea-like flowers of meadow vetchling are conspicuous in grassland or grassy hedgerows. They are 10–20mm long and grow in clusters of 5–12 at the extremity of each vertical flower-stalk, which is perfectly square in cross-section. Some stems may run along the ground, clinging to low vegetation with twisting tendrils. The paired leaves are narrow and pointed. Flowers May–August.

69 Is the plant a climber?

(from 67)

Answer 'Yes' if it grows by twining itself around other vegetation or clinging to it. Answer 'No' if the stem is upright and self-supporting.

Yes 70   No 71

70 HONEYSUCKLE
(Lonicera periclymenum)

(from 69
and 275)

Honeysuckle almost always grows by twining its rough stem around nearby bushes or trees, but will sprawl along the ground if none is available. Its fragrant flowers (4–5cm long) grow in clusters of up to a dozen, all facing outward, and attached to their stalk by long tubes. The paired leaves are oval with pointed tips and have no teeth or lobes. Honeysuckle likes shade and is found in woodland, scrub or hedgerows. Flowers June–October.

71 Do the flowers have long spurs?

(from 69)

A glance at the illustration will make it easy for you to decide on your answer.

Yes 58   No 72

spur

72 YELLOW RATTLE
(*Rhinanthus minor*)

(from 71)

Yellow rattle almost always grows in grassland, usually in neglected meadows, sometimes in quite large patches. It may reach 60cm in height but is usually shorter (7–20cm). The two-lipped flowers, 1–1½cm long, are unusual in shape and have a conspicuous greeny-brown calyx. They grow in pairs in a loose cluster at the end of each stem, with two leaf-like bracts below each pair. The leaves are pointed and toothed. Flowers May–August.

73 How many petals has each flower?

(from 6)

Count the number of petals in each flower and choose your answer accordingly.

8–12   74
5   75
6   78
Over 12   81

74 | **LESSER CELANDINE**
(Ranunculus ficaria)

(from 73)

The well-known lesser celandine is one of the very first flowers to blossom. Its shiny yellow flowers ($1\frac{1}{2}$–5cm) are conspicuous in March and it continues in bloom till May. The number of pointed petals may vary from 8 to 12. Each flower grows singly on its own stalk. The leaves are shiny and heart-shaped or nearly round. This plant enjoys a damp site by a stream, or on a bank beside a ditch, but also thrives in woodland or by hedgerows.

75 | Do the flowers grow singly?

(from 73)

Answer 'Yes' if each flower is solitary, with its own stalk to itself. Answer 'No' if several flowers grow together in a cluster at the end of each stem.

Yes 76   No 77

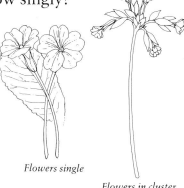

Flowers single

Flowers in cluster

76 | **PRIMROSE**
(Primula vulgaris)

(from 75)

The primrose is one of the best-known and best-loved flowers. It is often the very first to appear, sometimes blooming for Christmas. The flowers (2–3cm) are pale yellow and each has its long stalk, which rises from a rosette of roughly toothed, wrinkled leaves, smooth above and slightly hairy below. The primrose grows on banks, in woodland, at roadsides and in hedgerows. Flowers till May.

77 | COWSLIP
(Primula veris)
(from 75)

The cowslip is much the same colour as the primrose (see 76), but its flowers are smaller in diameter (8–12mm) and anything up to 30 of them (usually 8–12) dangle together from the end of each stem. The leaves are much like a primrose's, but both sides are hairy. Cowslips prefer open ground and usually grow in meadows or grazing fields. Flowers April–May.

78 | Do the flowers grow singly?
(from 73)

Answer 'Yes' if each flower is solitary, with its own stalk to itself. Answer 'No' if several flowers grow together in a cluster at the end of each stem.

Yes 79   No 80

Wild daffodil

79 | WILD DAFFODIL
(Narcissus pseudonarcissus)
(from 78)

The all-yellow wild daffodil is similar in shape to the well-known cultivated species, with its six regularly radiating petals ($3\frac{1}{2}$–5cm) and the familiar 'trumpet' in the centre. The whole plant is hairless. Long, narrow leaves rise from its base, enveloping the stem, which bears a single flower. This is a plant of grassland and woodland. Flowers February–April.

Bog asphodel

80 BOG ASPHODEL
(Narthecium ossifragum)

(from 78)

This plant, as its name indicates, is to be found only in bogland or on moors. It appears in July as a small spike of fragrant, bright yellow flowers (1–1½cm) growing at the extremity of the erect stems, with grass-like leaves rising from their bases. Blooms till September, when the flowers become more orange-coloured. (See opposite.)

81 Are the leaves hairy?

(from 73)

Answer 'Yes' if the leaves are covered in short, stiff bristly hairs. Otherwise answer 'No'.

Yes 82   No 83

82 CAT'S-EAR
(Hypochoeris radicata)

(from 81)

Cat's-ear is extremely similar to autumnal hawkbit and the same description applies (see 85), except that the flowers tend to be larger (2½–4cm) and the leaves, which are less narrow, are quite noticeably bristly. The species is found in grassland, wasteland and at roadsides. Flowers June–September.

83 Are the flowers solitary?

(from 81)

Answer 'Yes' if each flower is solitary, with its own stem to itself. Answer 'No' if each stem bears two or more flowers.

Yes 84   No 85

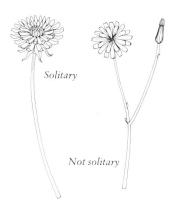

Solitary

Not solitary

84 DANDELION
(Taraxacum officinale)
(from 83)

Almost everyone already knows the dandelion. Its large, bright yellow flowerheads (3–7cm) grow singly at the ends of thick, hollow stems. The leaves are deeply lobed and pointed. Beneath each flowerhead is a ring of bracts (like very small leaves), which at first embrace the flower but soon turn downward. This very common flower grows in open meadows or by hedgerows or roadsides. Flowers March–October.

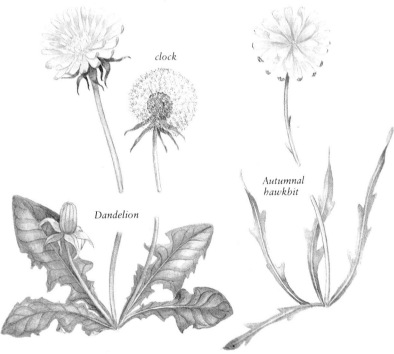

clock

Autumnal hawkbit

Dandelion

85 AUTUMNAL HAWKBIT
(Leontodon autumnalis)
(from 83)

The flowerheads are like those of a dandelion (see 84) but smaller (1–3½cm). They have fewer petal-like florets, and their undersides are often tinged with red. They grow in very loose clusters from the ends of branching stems. If the stem is cut or broken, it exudes a milky liquid. The leaves, which are narrow and lobed, are almost always hairless. Grows in grassland and wasteland. Flowers July–September.

86 COLT'S-FOOT
(Tussilago farfara)

(from 6)

Colt's-foot is specially welcome because it flowers before almost any other species. If a fine day comes in early February, clumps of it begin to appear in bloom. Until its flowers are over, no true leaves are grown. Each flowerhead grows singly, at the end of its erect stem, and looks quite like a small dandelion ($1\frac{1}{2}$–3cm). When the basal leaves appear, they may be very large (up to 30cm). They are toothed; and shaped something like a colt's foot, which gives the plant its name. Usually grows on wasteland and by roadsides. Flowers February–April.

87 Is the plant growing in water?

(from 1)

Answer 'Yes' if the lower part of the stem, or all the stem, is submerged in water. Answer 'No' if the plant is growing on dry land, or if only the roots are submerged.

Yes 88   No 93

88 How many petals has each flower?

(from 87)

Count the number of petals in each flower and choose your answer accordingly.

3 or 6 89
5 91
Over 10 92

89 What size are the flowers?

(from 88)

Measure the diameter of an average-sized flower to decide the right answer.

About 5mm 90
Over 20mm 285

90 CANADIAN WATERWEED
(Elodea canadensis)

(from 89
and 317)

This plant may grow in almost any
water, even quite fast-moving rivers.
Often the whole of it is submerged
apart from any flowers and their
stalks. The flowers have three petals
and three rather similar sepals, which
may lead beginners to think it is 6-
petalled. They grow singly and are
very small (5mm), regular and tinged
with pink. The pointed leaves grow
in close whorls of 3 around their
stems. Flowers May–October.

91 THREAD-LEAVED
WATER-CROWFOOT
(from 88) *(Ranunculus trichophyllus)*

The flowers and flower-stalks of this
plant are usually the only parts to
appear above the water. Each flower
(8–10mm) has 5 regular petals,
which do not touch one another. Its
centre is yellow. The few thread-like
leaves are submerged. Grows in
slow-moving rivers, ponds and
ditches. Flowers May–June.

92 WHITE WATER-LILY
(Nymphaea alba)

(from 88)

This handsome flower is quite
unmistakable, with its two rings of
sharply pointed petals and its great
size (10–20cm). The flowers
normally float on the water, as do the
large, glossy, heart-shaped leaves.
White water-lilies grow in slow-
moving rivers, or in standing water
with a depth of up to 300cm. Flowers
June–September.

93 How do the leaves grow?

(from 87)

Leaves are described as being alternate, opposite, whorled or basal, depending on how they grow along their stem or stalk.

Alternate leaves grow singly, on alternating sides of the stem. Opposite leaves are in pairs, and whorled leaves in groups of 3 or more around it. Choose 'Basal only'

if all the leaves grow at the very base of the plant.

The drawings should make your choice quite easy.

Alternate 94
Opposite or whorled 141
Basal only 171

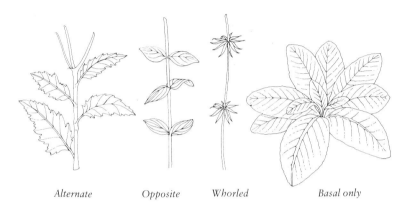

Alternate   *Opposite*   *Whorled*   *Basal only*

94 Are the flowers in umbels?

(from 93)

Flowers are said to be in umbels if they grow at the end of stalks (all much the same length) that radiate like the spokes of an umbrella from the very end of the stem.
Answer 'Yes' if the flowers are so arranged. Otherwise answer 'No'.
(The small leaf-like growth at the base of some umbels is called a bract.)

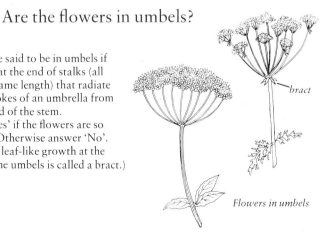

bract

Flowers in umbels

Yes 95
No 110

Are the leaflets broad and undivided?

(from 94)

All flowers in this section have composite leaves, which means that each leaf is composed of several smaller leaflets. Answer 'Yes' if the leaflets are quite broad (at least one-third of their length) and, though they may be toothed or lobed, are not deeply divided. Otherwise answer 'No'.

Yes 96   No 101

Are the leaflets lobed?

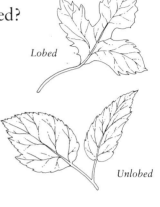

Lobed

Unloved

(from 95)

Answer 'Yes' if each leaflet is quite deeply lobed. Answer 'No' if the leaflets are toothed but without lobes.

Yes 97   No 98

97   **HOGWEED**
          (Heracleum sphondylium)

(from 96)

The broad, lobed leaflets of the hogweed are quite unlike those of any other plant in this section. The whole plant is stiffly hairy. The flowers are relatively large (5–10mm) in a compound umbel (5–15cm). The hollow stem may reach a height of 200cm. Hogweed grows in woodland, along hedgerows and in grassland. Flowers June–September.

98   Is the flowerhead yellowish?

(from 96)

Answer 'Yes' if each little flower has 5 protruding yellow stamens, so that the entire flowerhead has a slight yellowish tinge. Otherwise answer 'No'.

Yes 99   No 100

protruding stamens

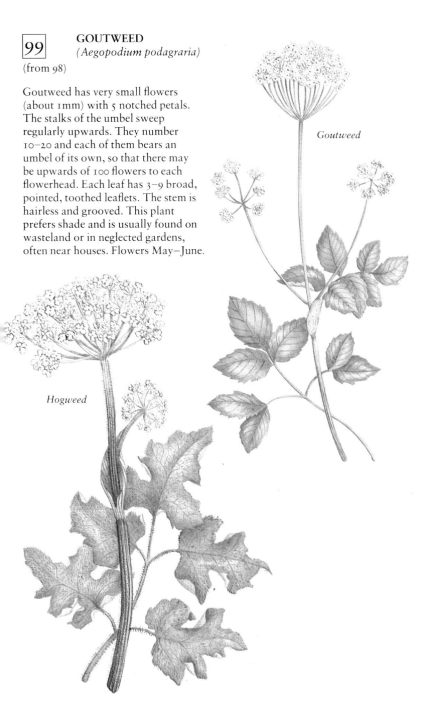

99   **GOUTWEED**
      (Aegopodium podagraria)

(from 98)

Goutweed has very small flowers
(about 1mm) with 5 notched petals.
The stalks of the umbel sweep
regularly upwards. They number
10–20 and each of them bears an
umbel of its own, so that there may
be upwards of 100 flowers to each
flowerhead. Each leaf has 3–9 broad,
pointed, toothed leaflets. The stem is
hairless and grooved. This plant
prefers shade and is usually found on
wasteland or in neglected gardens,
often near houses. Flowers May–June.

Goutweed

Hogweed

100 WILD ANGELICA
(Angelica sylvestris)

(from 98)

This plant prefers shade and often grows on damp ground or beside a river or lake. The umbel is composed of up to 30 stalks, which grow rather irregularly, so that the flowerhead is not flat topped. Each stalk bears an umbel of its own. The flowers (about 2mm) have 5 notched petals. Angelica, which may reach a height of 200cm, is almost completely hairless. Its large leaves have sheaths at their bases, where they embrace the stem. There are extra large leaves at the base of the plant. Flowers July–September.

101 Are there bracts under the umbels?

(from 95)

A bract looks exactly like a small leaf. Answer 'Yes' if at least one bract is growing just under each umbel. Otherwise answer 'No'.

Yes | 102 | No | 107 |

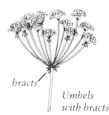

bracts
*Umbels
with bracts*

*Umbels
without bracts*

102 Are the bracts conspicuous?

(from 101)

Answer 'Yes' if the bracts are large and unmistakable. Answer 'No' if they are so small that you might nearly miss them.

Yes | 103 | No | 104 |

| 103 |

(from 102)

WILD CARROT
(Daucus carota)

The flowerhead of wild carrot is a compound umbel, which means that each main umbel is itself composed of many secondary umbels. The central flower of each of the secondary umbels is usually tinged with pink. There are very conspicuous, deeply-divided bracts, which look like leaves, immediately under each main umbel. The leaves, also deeply divided, are sheathed where they meet the erect, stiffly hairy stem. This plant often grows by the sea-shore, or in grassy places anywhere. Flowers June to August.

| 104 |

(from 102)

Is the stem covered with purple spots?

Answer 'Yes' if the stem is quite liberally covered with purple spots or blotches (see illustration to 105).

Answer 'No' if there is no such purple colouring.

Yes | 105 | No | 106 |

| 105 |

(from 104)

HEMLOCK
(Conium maculatum)

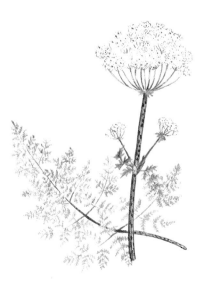

This extremely poisonous plant may grow to a great height (200–300cm) and develops a very thick, hollow stem. The entire plant is hairless. The flowers grow in a compound umbel, meaning that each main umbel is itself composed of secondary umbels. The individual flowers are small (2mm) and have 5 petals. The bracts beneath each main umbel are also small. The leaves are compound and fern-like. Hemlock often grows quite near water or on damp ground, usually wasteland. Flowers June–July.

106

(from 104)

UPRIGHT HEDGE-PARSLEY
(Torilis japonica)

This plant grows to a height of 50–100cm. It has a slender, erect stem. The umbels are quite small, with 5–12 main flower-stalks. There are small bracts under each main umbel. The flowers are tinged with purple. Each leaf is composed of several deeply divided leaflets, which grow in pairs along their stalks. The whole plant is hairy. It usually grows on roadsides, but also occurs in wasteland or by hedgerows. Flowers July–September.

107

When does it flower?

(from 101)

Of the two most likely remaining species, one blooms from April till mid-June; the other does not come out till late June or early July. Choose your answer accordingly.

April–June 108
July–August 109

108

(from 107)

COW PARSLEY
(Anthriscus sylvestris)

This is probably the commonest of all the plants with umbels and it is the first of them to come out, usually in April. The flowers are relatively large (2–4mm) and somewhat irregular in shape. The umbels are 2–6cm in diameter. The compound leaves are very deeply divided. The stem of cow parsley is erect and grooved, and reaches a height of over 100cm. Usually grows on roadsides or in hedgerows. Flowers April–June.

109

(from 107)

BURNET-SAXIFRAGE
(Pimpinella saxifraga)

Rather similar to cow parsley (see 108) apart from its later flowering. The 5-petalled flowers tend to be more regular and smaller (2mm). They are again in compound umbels, 2–5cm in diameter. All the leaves are compound. The leaflets of those on the stem are very deeply divided, but those at the base of the plant are broader. The ridged, erect stems have rough hairs and grow up to 100cm high. Found in dry grassland. Flowers July–August.

110 ## Are the flowers bell-shaped?

(from 94)

Answer 'Yes' if the petals are fused together so that they cannot easily be distinguished, and the flowers are shaped more or less like a bell or funnel. Answer 'No' if each petal is clearly distinct down to its base.

Yes 111   No 115

Bell-shaped

Funnel-shaped

111 ## Is the plant a climber?

(from 110)

Answer 'Yes' if it grows by twining itself around other vegetation. Answer 'No' if the stem is upright and self-supporting.

Yes 112   No 114

112 ## How big are the flowers?

(from 111)

Measure the diameter of an average-sized flower to decide on the answer.

2cm 212

$3\frac{1}{2}$–7cm 113

HEDGE BINDWEED
(Calystegia sepium)

113

(from 112)

The bindweeds are at once
distinguished, with their twisty stems
twining strongly round nearby
vegetation. The flowers of the hedge
bindweed ($3\frac{1}{2}$–7cm) are pure white,
with no distinct petals. They grow
singly on quite long stalks. The
whole plant is hairless. The glossy,
dark green leaves are shaped like
arrowheads. Grows in hedgerows
and woodland margins. Flowers
July–September.

Hedge bindweed

Common comfrey

*colour
variants*

COMMON COMFREY
(Symphytum officinale)

114

(from 111,
209 and 303)

The flowers of the comfrey may be
bluish-purple, pink or white, but the

fully-opened flowers on one plant are
always the same colour. They usually

hang downwards, growing in small clusters at the end of the branched stems. The whole plant is noticeably hairy. The leaves are quite long and narrow, and grow alternately. Comfrey likes damp places and is often found growing by rivers and streams. Flowers May–June.

How many petals has each flower?

(from 110)

Count the number of petals, or petal-like sepals, in each flower and choose your answer accordingly.

4 | 116 |
5 | 120 |
6 or more | 134 |

What size are the flowers?

(from 115)

Measure the diameter of an average-sized flower and choose your answer accordingly.

25–40mm | 117 |
12–18mm | 310 |
6mm | 118 |
2½mm | 119 |

lilac form

WILD RADISH
(*Raphanus raphanistrum*)

(from 116, 20 and 308)

The flowers of wild radish may be white, yellow or lilac, often with darker veins, but the flowers of any given specimen are always the same colour. The 4 petals are entirely separate and do not touch each other. The flowers are in loose clusters and the lower ones develop into long, upright seed-pods while the upper ones are still in flower. The upper leaves are toothed and sometimes lobed. This is a common weed of arable land. Flowers May–September.

The large, glossy leaves of garlic mustard have long stems and are strongly toothed. The flowers are in clusters and quite small (6mm) in relation to the plant's height (up to 120cm). The stem is straight and unbranched. Garlic mustard is virtually hairless and smells of garlic when crushed. It often grows beside walls, on the edge of woodland or in hedgerows. Flowers April–June.

This is one of the commonest flowers and is in bloom for nearly all the year. Its very small flowers (2–3mm) are regular and grow in clusters. They develop into heart-shaped seed-pods. Most of the leaves are at the base of the plant, and are usually deeply divided. The upper leaves, which embrace the stem, are neither divided nor toothed. Shepherd's-purse grows almost anywhere, but is very often found on wasteland or on roadsides.

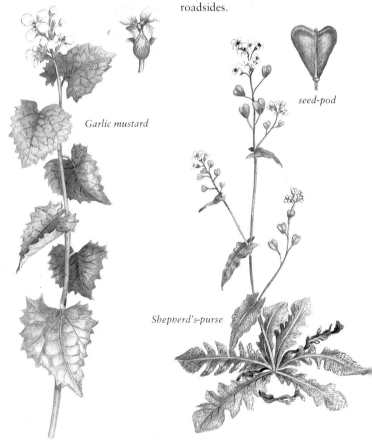

Garlic mustard

seed-pod

Shepherd's-purse

120 Is the stem thorny?

(from 115)

Answer 'Yes' if the stem and stalks have sharp thorns or spines. Answer 'No' if they are completely thornless.

Yes 121   No 123

121 Are the petals heart-shaped?

(from 120)

Answer 'Yes' if each petal has an indentation, making it appear heart-shaped. Otherwise answer 'No'.

Yes 122   No 229

122 BURNET ROSE
(Rosa pimpinellifolia)

(from 121)

The petals of the burnet rose are pure white or creamy white without any pink or red. The flowers (2–4cm) are regular, with bright yellow stamens in their centre. The compound leaves have 5 or more narrow, toothed leaflets, arranged in pairs. The stem and stalks are thickly covered in sharp spines and thorns. This rose most often grows by the sea on sandy, grassy land, but also appears inland, on downs, heaths and scrubland. Flowers May–June.

123 Is the plant a climber?

(from 120)

Answer 'Yes' if it grows by twining round other vegetation. Answer 'No' if the stem is upright and self-supporting.

Yes 124   No 126

124 Are the leaves 5-lobed?

(from 123)

Answer 'Yes' if each leaf is divided into 5 lobes like the fingers of your hand. Otherwise answer 'No'.

Yes 362   No 125

5-lobed leaf

125 BLACK BINDWEED
(Fallopia convolvulus)

(from 124
and 246)

The twining black bindweed has very
small greenish-white or pinkish
flowers, which grow in little clusters
on stalks rising from the leaf-axils
(where the leaf-stalks join the stem).
The leaves are dark green, hairless
and glossy, with powdery white
undersides. They are shaped like
spearheads. The stem may reach a
length of over 100cm. The plant
often grows on wasteland or in
hedgerows. Flowers July–October.

126 Do the flowers grow in large clusters?

(from 123)

Answer 'Yes' if each flowerhead is a
large, compact cluster of many small
flowers. Answer 'No' if the flowers
grow in little groups of 1–6.

Yes 127

No 130

*Flowers in
large cluster*

*Flowers in
little groups*

Do the leaves have broad segments?

(from 126)

Answer 'Yes' if the divisions of each leaf are broad and flat. Answer 'No' if they are thin and fern-like.

Yes | 128 | No | 129 |

Broad flat leaflets

Thin fern-like leaflets

| 128 | **MEADOWSWEET**
(Filipendula ulmaria)

(from 127)

This plant prefers damp ground, and is most common in old meadowland, in pasture or by rivers. It is very conspicuous, reaching a height of over 100cm with large, dense clusters of creamy-white flowers which have a distinctive bittersweet smell. The stems and stalks are often reddish. The compound leaves have 5 or more strongly toothed leaflets. Flowers June–September.

| 129 | **YARROW**
(Achillea millefolium)

(from 127)

The yarrow's flowers (4–6mm) grow in smooth, flat-topped flowerheads, whose stalks do not all radiate from exactly the same point on the stem.

Meadowsweet

The erect stem is covered with soft hairs. All the leaves are very deeply divided and fern-like. Yarrow is to be found in grassland or wasteland, and grows in hedgerows and by roadsides. Flowers June–August.

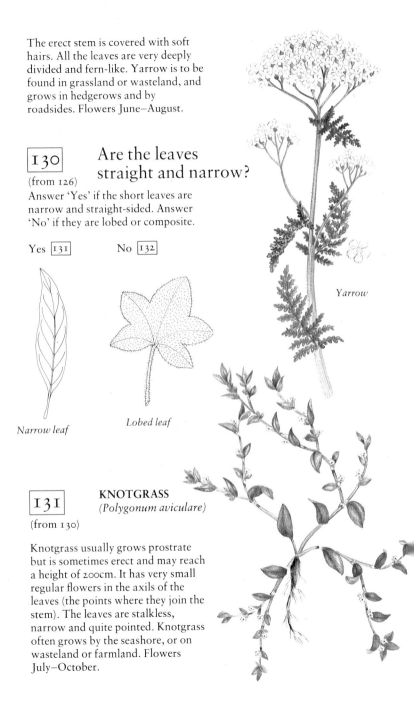

130 Are the leaves straight and narrow?

(from 126)

Answer 'Yes' if the short leaves are narrow and straight-sided. Answer 'No' if they are lobed or composite.

Yes 131   No 132

Narrow leaf

Lobed leaf

Yarrow

131 KNOTGRASS
(Polygonum aviculare)

(from 130)

Knotgrass usually grows prostrate but is sometimes erect and may reach a height of 200cm. It has very small regular flowers in the axils of the leaves (the points where they join the stem). The leaves are stalkless, narrow and quite pointed. Knotgrass often grows by the seashore, or on wasteland or farmland. Flowers July–October.

132 How big are the flowers?

(from 130)

Measure the diameter of an average-sized flower and choose your answer accordingly.

4–6mm 133
10–20mm 177

133 RUE-LEAVED SAXIFRAGE
(Saxifraga tridactylites)

(from 132)

This small plant, not usually more than 10cm high, has regular flowers (4–6mm) which grow in very loose clusters, each with a stalk of its own. Its lower leaves are quite large and deeply lobed, whilst those higher up the stem are smaller and undivided. The leaves and the stem, which is covered with sticky hairs, may be strongly tinged with red. The plant usually grows on walls or on sandy ground. Flowers April–June.

134 Are the flowers daisy-like?

(from 115)

Answer 'Yes' if the flowers look like large daisies, with white rays and a yellow centre. Otherwise answer 'No'.

Yes 135   No 138

135 Are the leaves very narrow?

(from 134)

Answer 'Yes' if all the leaves are divided into extremely narrow segments, little wider than threads. Answer 'No' if they are quite broad, despite being deeply lobed.

Yes 136   No 137

Very narrow leaf

Quite broad leaf

SCENTLESS MAYWEED
(Tripleurospermum inodorum)

Easily distinguished from the more common ox-eye daisy by its extremely narrow leaves, scentless mayweed is usually found as a weed of cultivated and waste ground. The flowers ($1\frac{1}{2}$–5cm) are solitary, each with its own long stalk. There is usually a leaf where the flower-stalk joins the stem. The whole plant is hairless. Flowers June–September.

Ox-eye daisy

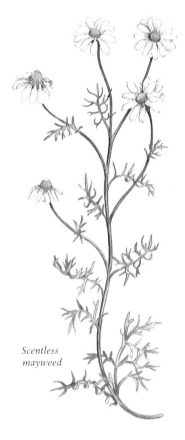

Scentless mayweed

OX-EYE DAISY
(Leucanthemum vulgare)

The ox-eye daisy's leaves are much broader than the scentless mayweed's. They are deeply lobed, dark green and stalkless. The whole plant is almost hairless. This well-known, easily recognizable flower grows in grassland or wasteland and blooms June–August.

Black bryony

138 Is it a climber?

(from 134)

Answer 'Yes' if the plant grows by twining itself around other vegetation. Answer 'No' if the stem is upright and self-supporting.

Yes 139   No 140

139 **BLACK BRYONY**
(Tamus communis)

(from 138
and 357)

The stem of black bryony twists firmly around the supporting vegetation. Its heart-shaped leaves are glossy and have quite long stalks. The flowers are small (4–5mm) and grow in little clusters where the leaf-stalks join the stem. Although they appear to have six petals, three of them are in fact sepals. Black bryony grows in hedgerows, by woodland margins and in scrubland. Flowers May–July.

140 **GREATER BUTTERFLY ORCHID**
(Platanthera chlorantha)

(from 138)

The flowers of this orchid (18–23mm) are arranged in a loose spike. They are white, tinged with green, and very fragrant. There are two large, pointed leaves at the base of the plant, and smaller ones growing alternately along the erect stem. The whole plant is hairless. This orchid likes chalky ground and usually grows in woods and grassland. Flowers May–June.

(Note: the common spotted orchid

usually has pinkish flowers but sometimes they are white tinged with pink or occasionally pure white. If the above description does not seem correct, have a look at the spotted orchid – see 253.)

141 Are the flowers regular?

(from 93)
Answer 'Yes' if all the petals of each flower are equal in size and the same shape. Otherwise answer 'No'.

Yes 142   No 166

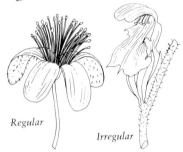

Regular

Irregular

142 How many petals has each flower?

(from 141)
Count the number of petals (or petal-like sepals) in each flower and choose your answer accordingly.

4 143
5 147
6–7 146

143 Are the leaves opposite or whorled?

(from 142)
Decide whether the leaves grow in opposing pairs along the stem, or whether they are in whorls around it.

Opposite 144
Whorled 145

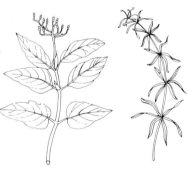

144 TRAVELLER'S-JOY
(Clematis vitalba)

(from 143)

The flowers (2cm) grow in a loose cluster on a stalk which arises from the point where the leaf-stalk joins the stem. The leaves are composite: each one has 3–5 pointed, usually toothed, leaflets growing in opposite pairs. The plant twines around the

Opposite   *Whorled*

surrounding vegetation for support. It grows on the edges of woods, in hedgerows and scrubland. Flowers July–August. (See opposite.)

GOOSEGRASS
(Galium aparine)

145

(from 143)

This plant, also known as cleavers, is a favourite in children's games because it sticks to clothes and hair with the tiny spines on its stems and fruits. It has extremely small flowers (2mm) in loose clusters on short stalks. Its very narrow leaves grow in whorls around its square stem. Sometimes it grows erect, but more often sprawls over nearby vegetation. Often found on wasteland, in hedgerows or on roadsides. Flowers June–August.

Goosegrass

WOOD ANEMONE
(Anemone nemorosa)

146

(from 142)

This is one of the first flowers to open in the springtime. Its solitary blooms (2–4cm) have 6–7 pure white sepals (which look exactly like petals). There is a whorl of deeply-divided leaves halfway up the stem. The whole plant is hairless. It is usually found in deciduous woodland. Flowers March–May.

Traveller's-joy

Wood anemone

Are the petals indented?

(from 142)

Answer 'Yes' if there is a clear indentation in each petal, so that it is either heart-shaped or deeply divided. Answer 'No' if the petals are rounded or pointed, without any such indentation.

Yes 148   No 159

Petals indented

Petals not indented

148   Does it have a square stem?

(from 147)

Answer 'Yes' if the stem is noticeably square-shaped in cross-section. Answer 'No' if it is rounded.

Yes 149   No 152

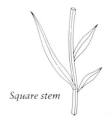

Square stem

149   How big are the flowers?

(from 148)

Measure the diameter of an average-sized flower and decide your answer accordingly.

5–12mm 150
Over 15mm 151

150   LESSER STITCHWORT
(Stellaria graminea)

(from 149)

The small flowers (5–12mm) have deeply divided petals. They grow on individual stalks, which rise from the points where the leaves join the stem.

The stalkless leaves are small, narrow and pointed. Grows in grassland or woodland. Flowers May–August. (See opposite.)

GREATER STITCHWORT
(Stellaria holostea)

(from 149)

Similar to lesser stitchwort (see 150)
but the flowers are larger (2–3cm) as
are the leaves. It is found in much the
same places, but tends to flower
sooner, in April–June.

Greater
stitchwort

Lesser
stitchwort

| 152 | How big are the flowers?

(from 148)
Measure the diameter of an average-
sized flower and decide your answer
accordingly.

Up to 15mm | 153 |
Over 18mm | 156 |

| 153 | Is the plant noticeably hairy?

(from 152)
Answer 'Yes' if the stem and leaves
are noticeably hairy. Answer 'No' if

they are hairless or nearly so.
Yes | 154 | No | 155 |

154

COMMON MOUSE-EAR
(Cerastium fontanum)

(from 153)

The leaves and stem of this common little plant are noticeably hairy. There is a pointed green sepal between each of the 5 deeply-notched petals in each flower. The flowers (10–15mm) grow in loose clusters. All the leaves are stalkless. Common mouse-ear may grow almost anywhere and flowers April–September.

155

CHICKWEED
(Stellaria media)

(from 153)

This plant has a weak stem and tends to sprawl over the ground. The flowers (8–10mm) have petals that are very deeply divided. There are prominent pointed sepals between the petals. The leaves are oval and pointed; the upper ones are stalkless but some of those at the base of the plant may have stalks. Chickweed is very common in gardens, fields and wasteland. Flowers all year.

156   Is the plant noticeably hairy?

(from 152)

Answer 'Yes' if the stem and leaves are noticeably hairy. Answer 'No' if they are almost or completely hairless, except perhaps for some light down.

Yes [157]   No [158]

157

WHITE CAMPION
(Silene alba)

(from 156)

The stem of white campion is usually branched and may reach almost 100cm in height. The few flowers ($2\frac{1}{2}$–3cm) have deeply notched petals and grow in small loose clusters. They usually open in the evenings. There is a prominent, green or brown calyx-tube under each flower. The pointed leaves are stalkless, except perhaps towards the base. This is quite a common weed of arable land and also grows in hedgerows and on wasteland. Flowers May–September.

White campion

158

BLADDER CAMPION
(Silene vulgaris)

(from 156)

This plant is very similar to white campion (see 157), but the flowers are smaller (15mm) and the swollen calyx-tube beneath each of them is even more conspicuous. It is found in much the same places but has a shorter flowering season, July–August.

159

(from 147)

Do the leaves grow in whorls?

Answer 'Yes' if the leaves are very narrow and grow in whorls along the stem. Answer 'No' if they are not noticeably narrow and grow along the stem in opposite pairs.

Yes 160   No 161

Bladder campion

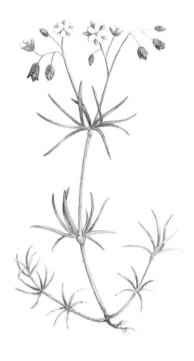

160 CORN SPURREY
(Spergula arvensis)

(from 159)

The very small white flowers
(4–7mm) grow in loose clusters at
the end of the stems, which are
branched and grow rather weakly.
The leaves are very unusual, being
arranged in whorls and needle-like.
The whole plant is usually sticky.
Most often seen in cornfields or on
wasteland; prefers sandy soil.
Flowers June–August.

161 Are the leaves hairy?

(from 159)

Answer 'Yes' if the leaves are
noticeably covered in hairs. Answer
'No' if they are completely or nearly
hairless.

Yes 162   No 163

162 THYME-LEAVED SANDWORT
(Arenaria serpyllifolia)

(from 161)

This plant is distinguished by its very
small, stalkless leaves, and by its
small flowers (5–6mm). The
conspicuous pointed sepals are rather
longer than the petals and alternate
between them. There are 1–2 flowers
on individual stalks towards the ends
of the branching stems. Thyme-
leaved sandwort often grows on
walls and is also found in grassland,
on arable ground and on wasteland.
Flowers June–August.

(from 161)

Answer 'Yes' if the plant is growing on or near a seaside beach or coastal sand dunes. Otherwise answer 'No'.

Yes 164   No 165

164   **SEA SANDWORT** *(Honkenya peploides)*

(from 163)

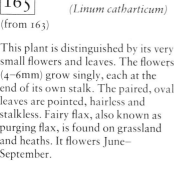

This plant almost always grows by the sea, where it may be found creeping among stones and shingle or in sand. It is completely hairless with rather fleshy, pointed, stalkless leaves. The flowers are similar to those of thyme-leaved sandwort (see 162) but rather larger (6–10mm). They are solitary, growing on short stalks from the ends of the stem, or from the points on the stem where pairs of leaves grow. Flowers May–August.

165   **FAIRY FLAX** *(Linum catharticum)*

(from 163)

This plant is distinguished by its very small flowers and leaves. The flowers (4–6mm) grow singly, each at the end of its own stalk. The paired, oval leaves are pointed, hairless and stalkless. Fairy flax, also known as purging flax, is found on grassland and heaths. It flowers June–September.

166   Are the leaves more than 10mm long?

(from 141)

Measure the length of an average leaf and choose your answer accordingly.   Yes 167   No 170

167
(from 166)

Does each flower have two divided petals?

Answer 'Yes' if the flowers are very small and have only two petals each, deeply divided so that there may appear to be 4. Otherwise answer 'No'.

Yes 168   No 169

2 divided petals

Enchanter's-nightshade

168
(from 167)

ENCHANTER'S-NIGHTSHADE
(Circaea lutetiana)

The very small flowers (4–8mm) grow in a loose spike. The plant is erect and the stem slightly hairy. The oval, pointed leaves are in opposite pairs; they have shallow teeth and are stalked. Enchanter's-nightshade is found in woods or hedgerows. Flowers June–August.

White dead-nettle

169
(from 167)

WHITE DEAD-NETTLE
(Lamium album)

White dead-nettle looks like a common stinging nettle, except for its pure white flowers, which grow in well-spaced whorls around its hairy stem. The toothed leaves are long and pointed. It may be found on wasteground, in hedgerows or by roadsides. Flowers April–October.

170

COMMON EYEBRIGHT
(Euphrasia nemorosa)

(from 166)

This is a small plant, seldom more than 20cm in height, with a branched stem. The flowers are mainly white, but tinged with yellow and purple. The small leaves are stalkless and regularly toothed. Eyebright grows in grassy places and flowers May–September.

171

Do the flowers grow singly?

(from 93)

Answer 'Yes' if each flower is solitary, with its own stalk or stem to itself. Answer 'No' if several or many flowers grow close together; the flower-stalks, if any, are very short.

(Note: the well-known clovers may at first appear to have flowers growing singly, but in fact each flowerhead is composed of many tiny flowers and you should answer 'No'.)

Yes 172   No 184

Single

Not single

172

Are the flowers regular?

(from 171)

Answer 'Yes' if all the petals of each flower are equal in size and the same shape. Otherwise answer 'No'.

Yes 173   No 183

173   How many petals has each flower?

(from 172)
Count the number of petals in each flower and choose your answer accordingly.

3 or 6 174
5 175
Over 6 182

174   SNOWDROP
(Galanthus nivalis)

(from 173)

The snowdrop is widely planted and only occasionally grows wild. It is specially welcome because it is one of the very first plants to appear in bloom in the early days of the year. The solitary, nodding flowers (14–17mm) seem to have 6 petals – 3 larger ones in an outside ring and 3 smaller ones inside them – but the former are in fact sepals. The hairless leaves are long and narrow. Snowdrops grow in woodland and in hedgerows. They flower January–March.

175   Are the leaves in the form of trefoils?

(from 173)
Answer 'Yes' if each leaf is divided into 3 equal leaflets like a clover's. Such leaves are called trefoils. Answer 'No' if the leaves are simple and undivided.

Yes 176   No 181

Trefoil

Simple leaf

Are the leaflets toothed?

(from 175)

Examine the edges of the leaflets and answer 'Yes' if they are quite clearly toothed. Answer 'No' if they are smooth and toothless.

Yes | 177 | No | 180 |

Toothed   *Untoothed*

Are the petals rounded?

(from 176 and 132)

Answer 'Yes' if the petals of each flower are unmistakably rounded. Answer 'No' if they have a small indentation so that they are heart-shaped.

Yes | 178 | No | 179 |

Rounded   *Heart-shaped*

WILD STRAWBERRY
(Fragaria vesca)

(from 177)

The wild strawberry is best known for its delicious fruit, which resembles the well-known garden varieties but is very much smaller (less than 10mm). The flowers (12–18mm) are perfectly regular. It is usually found on shady banks, woodland edges and hedgerows. Flowers May–June.

179 BARREN STRAWBERRY
(Potentilla sterilis)

(from 177)

This plant is almost identical to the wild strawberry (see 178) except for the shape of its petals and its failure to bear conspicuous fruit. It flowers sooner, from March to June.

180 WOOD-SORREL
(Oxalis acetosella)

(from 176)

The wood-sorrel's leaves grow singly on the ends of long stalks, which rise from the base of the plant. The 3 equal leaflets making up each leaf are noticeably indented so that they are heart-shaped. The flowers (10–25mm), which also grow singly, are perfectly regular and usually drooping. The whole plant is hairless. Wood-sorrel almost always grows in deciduous woodland. Flowers April–May.

181 GRASS-OF-PARNASSUS
(Parnassia palustris)

(from 175)

This plant of the fens and marshes has erect stems bearing single flowers ($1\frac{1}{2}$–3cm), which are white with yellow centres. The heart-shaped, hairless leaves are also single, each with its own long stalk, rising from the base. There is also, usually, a single stalkless leaf, less than half-way up the flower-stem. Flowers July–October.

182

DAISY
(Bellis perennis)

(from 173)

The daisy is perhaps the best-known of all wild flowers. Its small white flowers ($1\frac{1}{2}$–3cm), yellow-centred and tipped with scarlet, grow singly on delicate stems. The short-stalked leaves are bluntly toothed, and, like the stems, they are hairy. Daisies grow on lawns and grassland. They flower March–October.

183

LORDS-AND-LADIES
(Arum maculatum)

(from 172)

This plant is immediately recognizable because of its extremely unusual flowerhead. The true flowers are very small and hidden at the base of the poker-like flower-spike, surrounded by the conspicuous, greenish-white flower-hood, which is erect, pointed and 15–25cm in length. The shiny, hairless leaves grow on long stalks from the base. Lords-and-ladies, also known as cuckoo-pint, grows in woods and hedgerows. Flowers April–May.

184

(from 171)

Does it have rounded flowerheads?

Answer 'Yes' if the plant is a clover, with many very small flowers growing close together in a rounded flowerhead. Otherwise answer 'No'.

Yes 185

No 186

Rounded flowerhead

185

WHITE CLOVER
(Trifolium repens)

(from 184)

This well-known little flower is completely hairless. The leaves are very regular trefoils, each composed of 3 rounded, indented leaflets. The flowerheads grow from long, leafless stalks; they turn brown from the bases upward. White clover puts out a long, creeping stem, which may take root at intervals. It is found on lawns and grassland. Flowers June–September.

186

Are the leaves sticky?

(from 184)
Answer 'Yes' if the leaves are fringed with long red sticky glands. Otherwise answer 'No'.

Yes 187   No 188

187

ROUND-LEAVED SUNDEW
(Drosera rotundifolia)

(from 186)

This little plant's most conspicuous feature is its small, round, fleshy leaves, which are covered in red glands. They grow on individual stalks. The tiny flowers are in a long spike at the end of each flower-stalk. They are perfectly regular with 5–6 pointed white petals, alternating with the same number of noticeable green sepals. This is a plant of moorland, marsh and bogland. It flowers June–August.

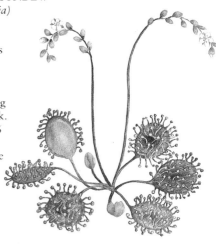

188   Are the leaves toothed?

(from 186)

Answer 'Yes' if the leaves are toothed
all round their margin. Answer 'No'
if they are quite smooth.

Yes 290   No 189

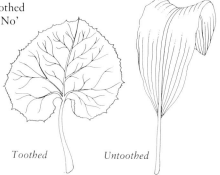

Toothed   *Untoothed*

189   Are the flowers sweet-smelling?

(from 188)

Answer 'Yes' if they are noticeably
sweet-scented. Answer 'No' if the
whole plant smells strongly of garlic.   Yes 190   No 191

190   **LILY-OF-THE-VALLEY**
(Convallaria majalis)

(from 189)

This plant is more often cultivated in
gardens, but also grows truly wild in
dry woodland. Each stem bears a
long cluster of 6–12 pure white,
drooping, bell-shaped flowers, all
facing the same way. The pointed
leaves, which are stalked and
hairless, grow in pairs at the base of
each stem. Flowers May–June.

flower

berry

(from 189)

191 RAMSONS
(Allium ursinum)

The star-like, pure white flowers grow singly on short radiating stalks at the end of each stem. The broad, pointed leaves are on individual stalks, arising from the base of the plant, which has a strong smell of garlic. It grows in woods and hedgerows. Flowers April–June.

192 How do the leaves grow?

(from 1)

Leaves are described as being alternate, opposite, whorled or basal, depending on how they grow along their stem or stalk.

Alternate leaves grow singly, on alternating sides of the stalk. Opposite leaves are in pairs, and whorled leaves in groups of 3 or more around it. Choose 'Basal only' if all the leaves grow at the very base of the plant.

The drawings should make your choice quite easy.

Alternate 193
Opposite or whorled 255
Basal only 281

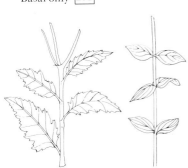

Alternate   *Opposite*   *Whorled*   *Basal only*

193   Are the flowers thistle-like?

(from 192)

Ignore the leaves and stem (which may or may not be prickly) and examine one of the flowerheads. Answer 'Yes' if it has the well-known appearance of a member of the thistle family, with no obvious petals but a mass of purple florets (see illustration) which grow upwards, very close together, from a more or less rounded base. This base is known as the involucre. Answer 'No' in all other cases.

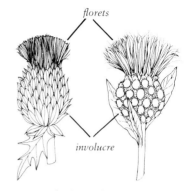

florets

involucre

Thistle-like flowers

Yes 194   No 205

194   Are the leaves prickly?

(from 193)

This question needs no elaboration.   Yes 195   No 202

195   Is the stem spiny?

(from 194)

Answer 'Yes' if the upright stem of the plant is covered with sharp spines or prickles for all or almost all its length. Answer 'No' if it is spineless.

Yes 196   No 201

196   Is the involucre very sharp and spiny?

(from 195)

The involucre is the lower part of the flowerhead, from which the florets grow upward. Answer 'Yes' if it is large and covered with long, sharp spines. Otherwise answer 'No'.

Yes 197   No 198

Involucre sharp and spiny

Spear thistle

Marsh thistle

197 SPEAR THISTLE
(Cirsium vulgare)

(from 196)

Spear thistle is best distinguished by
its extra large, very spiny involucre
(see 196). It grows taller than most
other thistles, up to 150cm, and its
leaves and stems are also extremely
spiny. The undersides of the leaves,
which are deeply lobed and pointed,
are often whitish with soft hairs. The
flowerheads either grow singly or in
small open clusters of 2–5. Spear
thistles grow in grassland, wasteland
or on roadsides. They flower July–
October.

198 Do the flower-
heads grow in
tight clusters?

(from 196)

Answer 'Yes' if most of the
flowerheads grow in quite a tight
cluster at the top of the stem. Answer
'No' if they are in an open cluster of
3–5 flowerheads, each with its own
noticeable stalk.

Yes 199   No 200

199 MARSH THISTLE
(Cirsium palustre)

(from 198)

As its name implies, this very prickly
thistle prefers a damp site, but it also
grows in quite dry fields, hedgerows
and woodland. It has relatively small
flowerheads (1–1½cm), growing in
close clusters at the top of the stem or
stalks. The narrow leaves are lobed
and spiny; except at the base of the
plant they are stalkless. Flowers
July–September.

| 200 | **WELTED THISTLE**
(Carduus acanthoides)
(from 198)

This thistle is distinguished by the very fine white hairs on the undersides of its leaves and on its stem. It has quite large flowerheads ($1\frac{1}{2}$–$2\frac{1}{2}$cm). Their involucres (see 196) are covered with many pointed bracts but they are not spiny. The leaves are deeply lobed, stalkless and very prickly. This plant grows in wasteland, open woodland, hedgerows or often near water. Flowers June–August.

Welted thistle

Creeping thistle

| 201 | **CREEPING THISTLE**
(Cirsium arvense)
(from 195)

Creeping thistles spread rapidly and often form a dense patch in open grassland or wasteland. They send up many erect, branching stems, which end in open clusters of small, light purple flowerheads. The lobed leaves are less prickly than those of other common thistles; the upper ones are stalkless and embrace the stems. Flowers July–September.

(from 194)

Answer 'Yes' if the leaves are at least
three times as long as they are broad.
Otherwise answer 'No'.   Yes 203   No 204

Lesser burdock

Common knapweed

203   **COMMON KNAPWEED**
     (Centaurea nigra)

(from 202)

Common knapweeds look like
thistles without the prickles. They
have branching, erect stems, with a
single purple flowerhead at the end
of every branch. The many purple
florets arise from a spherical, dark
brown involucre (see 196). The
leaves are very narrow and pointed,
with occasional lobes. Usually found
on roadsides or in grassland. Flowers
June–September.

204   **LESSER BURDOCK**
     (Arctium minus)

(from 202)

The flowerheads resemble those of a
thistle, but the plant is at once
distinguished by its very broad
smooth leaves. They grow at
intervals on stalks from the erect,
reddish-coloured stem. The
flowerheads grow from short stalks
in open clusters. Lesser burdock may
reach a height of 150cm, when it
becomes quite bushy in appearance,
with very large leaves (up to 40cm
long) towards the base. Flowers
July–September.

(from 193)

Answer 'Yes' if the plant is a clover,
with many small flowers in a
compact, rounded flowerhead.
Otherwise answer 'No'.   Yes 206   No 207

206

RED CLOVER
(Trifolium pratense)

(from 205)

There is usually a flowerhead at the end of every stem, with a small pair of stalkless leaves immediately below it. The main leaves are stalked; each is composed of 3 separate leaflets, forming a trefoil. They are narrow and usually pointed. Red clover grows fairly erect and may reach a height of 60cm or more. It is found in grassland and hedgerows. Flowers May–September.

207

(from 205)

Are the petals fused together?

Answer 'Yes' if the petals are fused together so that they cannot easily be distinguished and the flower is shaped more or less like a bell, funnel or tube. Answer 'No' if each petal is clearly distinct down to its base.

Yes 208   No 216

Bell-shaped

Funnel-shaped

208

Is the plant hairy?

(from 207)

Answer 'Yes' if the leaves and stem are noticeably hairy. Answer 'No' if they are almost or completely hairless, though they may have some soft down.

Yes 209   No 211

Straight spike

Twisted spike

209 — Are the flowers in a straight, erect spike?

(from 208)

Answer 'Yes' if the stem bearing the flowers is straight and perfectly upright. Answer 'No' if the flowers are in a spirally twisted spike, at least when young.

Yes 210   No 114

210 FOXGLOVE
(Digitalis purpurea)

(from 209)

The well-known foxglove is easily recognized with its tall, erect stem, usually unbranched, and its many purple, bell-shaped flowers. It sometimes reaches a height of 150cm. The hairy leaves are toothed and have short stalks. Foxgloves usually grow in woodland. They flower June–August.

211 — Is the plant a climber?

(from 208)

Answer 'Yes' if it grows by twining itself around other vegetation. Answer 'No' if the stem is upright and self-supporting.

Yes 212   No 213

212 FIELD BINDWEED
(Convolvulus arvensis)

(from 211 and 112)

Field bindweed is unmistakable as it climbs and twists with its pink or white flowers ($1\frac{1}{2}$–3cm) over and around nearby vegetation. The arrow-shaped leaves grow singly, each with its own short stalk. The flowers also have short stalks, and are either single or in pairs. Usually grows in gardens, where it is a common weed, or on farmland or in hedgerows. Flowers June–September.

Field bindweed

213

(from 211)

Is the flower 2-lipped?

Answer 'Yes' if the flower has 2 lips. Answer 'No' if it is bell-shaped and hangs down.

Yes 214   No 215

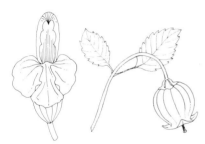

2-lipped flower   *Bell-shaped*

214

(from 213)

RED RATTLE
(Pedicularis palustris)

Red rattle

Red rattle grows with a single upright stem, which is usually purplish. The deeply divided leaves are its most noticeable feature. The pinkish-purple flowers are in a loose spike. Each of them has 2 lips; the upper one is very narrow, the lower one is broad. This plant, also known as marsh lousewort, has a liking for damp ground but will grow in grassland almost anywhere. Flowers May–September.

215
(from 213)

BILBERRY
(Vaccinium myrtillus)

Bilberries are best known for their delicious, rounded fruit, which turn purple-black when ripe. They develop from small flowers (4–6mm), which grow singly or in pairs on short stalks from the stems. The leaves, which are also short-stalked, are oval and toothed. Bilberries usually grow on moors and mountains, or in dry woodland. Flowers April–June.

fruit

216

(from 207)

How many petals has each flower?

Count the number of petals (or petal-like sepals) in each flower and choose your answer accordingly.

4   217
5   226
6   248
Not clear   226

217

(from 216)

Do the flowers grow singly?

Answer 'Yes' if each flower is solitary, with its own stem to itself. Answer 'No' if several or many flowers grow close together, and the flower-stalks are very short.

Yes   218   No   221

Flower single   *Flowers not single*

218   Are the petals scarlet?

(from 217)
Answer 'Yes' if the petals are scarlet,
usually with a black blotch at their
bases. Answer 'No' if they are a paler
orange-pink.

Yes 219   No 220

*seed
capsule*

Common poppy

*seed
capsule*

*flower
bud*

*flower
bud*

Long-headed poppy

219   COMMON POPPY
(Papaver rhoeas)

(from 218)

This poppy is extremely distinctive,
with its large, scarlet flowers
(7–10cm) which have delicate petals
and grow singly on long stems. The
leaves have deep lobes and are
almost stalkless. The smooth seed
capsule is noticeably rounded, unlike
the long-headed poppy (see 220).
Seldom seen in cornfields nowadays,
it is found growing on roadsides, on
wasteland and along the edges of
arable ground. Flowers June–
August.

220   LONG-HEADED POPPY
(Papaver dubium)

(from 218)

Similar to the common poppy (see
219) apart from its paler, smaller
flowers (3–7cm) and its more
elongated seed capsule.

221

(from 217)

Is the plant growing by the seaside?

Answer 'Yes' if it is growing in sand or shingle not far from the sea. Otherwise answer 'No'.

Yes 222   No 223

222

SEA ROCKET
(Cakile maritima)

(from 221)

This hairless, fleshy plant grows untidily on the seashore. Its stems sprawl along the beach, or along sand dunes or shingle, then rise to bear small clusters of flowers (1–2cm) and deeply divided leaves. The upper leaves are stalkless; the lower ones have short stalks. Flowers June–August.

223

(from 221)

Are the leaves composite?

Answer 'Yes' if each leaf is composed of several separate leaflets. Answer 'No' if the leaves, though they may be deeply divided, are each single and independent.

Yes 224   No 225

Composite   Single

224

COMMON FUMITORY
(Fumaria officinalis)

(from 223)

The flowers of fumitory (7–10mm long) are in a long spike at the end of the stem, with about 20 tube-like blossoms in each spike. Sometimes the plant grows erect, but more usually it twines itself around nearby vegetation. The fruit is green and spherical. Usually grows on arable land, but is also found on roadsides and wasteland. Flowers May–October. (See opposite.)

225

ROSEBAY WILLOWHERB
(Epilobium angustifolium)

(from 223)

This tall, erect plant bears a family
likeness to the two other willowherbs
covered in this book (see 265) but the
two upper petals of each flower are
slightly larger than the two lower
ones and the leaves are alternate. The
flowers (2–3cm) are rose-purple,
with narrow purple sepals between
the petals. They form a long
conspicuous spike. The leaves are
long and narrow. Often found on
waste ground, railway sidings or
bombsites, but also in woodland and
on roadsides. Flowers July–
September.

226

Are the leaves composite?

(from 216)

Answer 'Yes' if each leaf is composed
of several separate leaflets, which
may be rounded or pointed. Answer
'No' if the leaves, though they may
be deeply lobed, are each single and
independent.

Yes 227   No 240

*Rosebay
willowherb*

*Common
fumitory*

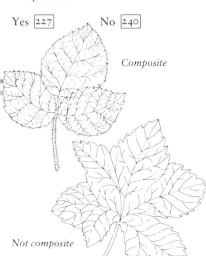

Composite

Not composite

Are the stems thorny?

(from 226)
Answer 'Yes' if all the stems are very noticeably covered with sharp thorns. Answer 'No' if they are thornless.

Yes 228   No 231

Are the petals pointed?

(from 227)
Answer 'Yes' if each petal comes to a point. Choose 'No' if each has a noticeable indentation, so that it is more or less heart-shaped.

Yes 229   No 230

Pointed   *Heart-shaped*

Bramble

229 BRAMBLE
(Rubus fruticosus)

(from 228 and 121)

There are many different brambles, all generally similar. The differences are too minor and complex for listing in this book. The well-known blackberry is typical of all of them, with its pink or white flowers (2–3cm), its thorny, arching stems, and above all its delicious fruit, which ripens from green to red to black. Brambles grow in hedgerows, on waste ground and in woodland. They flower May–September.

230 DOG ROSE
(Rosa canina)

(from 228)

Dog rose is very conspicuous, as it climbs over nearby vegetation with its handsome pink flowers (4–5cm), each of which has 5 heart-shaped petals. The composite leaves have 5–7 toothed leaflets, which are usually hairless, as is the thorny stem. The fruit is the well-known scarlet hip. Dog roses grow in hedgerows and woodland. They flower June–July.

Dog rose

| 231 | Is the plant a climber? |

(from 227)

Answer 'Yes' if it grows by twining itself around other vegetation. Answer 'No' if the stem is upright and self-supporting.

Yes 232   No 233

232	**COMMON VETCH**
(from 231)	*(Vicia sativa)*
	BUSH VETCH
	(Vicia sepium)

These two purple vetches are similar and it is best to take them together. The main difference is that the flowers of common vetch usually grow singly or in pairs whilst bush vetch's are in small clusters of 2–6. Both have tendrils at their leaf tips, enabling them to clamber round nearby vegetation, and 3–9 pairs of leaflets in each leaf, forming a regular pattern. Both plants are found in grassland and hedgerows. They flower May–September.

Note that another common member of the family, tufted vetch, has much bluer flowers and is not therefore included in this section (see 330).

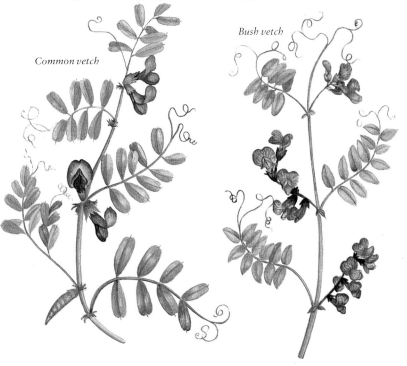

Common vetch

Bush vetch

233
(from 231)

Are the flowers shaped like those of a pea?

Answer 'Yes' if the irregular flowers are shaped like a pea's (see illustration). Otherwise answer 'No'.

Yes 234   No 235

Pea-like flower

234
RESTHARROW
(Ononis repens)
(from 233)

The stems of restharrow lie creeping along the ground, except towards the ends which usually turn upwards to bear the flowers. These grow on short stalks from the points in the stem where the leaves join it. The toothed leaves may grow singly, in pairs or in threes. The whole plant is hairy. It often grows on sand dunes by the sea, but also in grassland or scrub. Flowers June–September.

235
Are the leaflets opposite?
(from 233)

Answer 'Yes' if the leaflets are borne in opposite pairs along the leaf-stalk. Answer 'No' if they radiate from the tip of the leaf-stalk like the fingers of your hand.

Yes 236   No 239

Opposite leaflets

Radiating leaflets

Do the flowers hang down?

(from 235)
Answer 'Yes' if the flowers hang on long, slender stalks. Answer 'No' if they are borne on straight stalks and face upwards.

Yes | 237 | No | 238 |

| 237 | **WATER AVENS**
(Geum rivale)

(from 236)

The flowers hang singly, each from its own slender stalk towards the end of the stem. They are pinkish with 5 rounded petals, surrounded by 5 prominent purple sepals. The composite leaves are composed of

toothed leaflets in opposite pairs; the end leaflet is the largest. The whole plant is hairy. Water avens grows in damp woodlands as well as in shady places near water and in hedgerows. Flowers May–September.

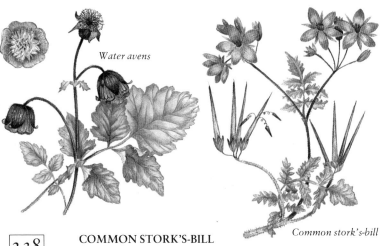

Water avens

Common stork's-bill

| 238 | **COMMON STORK'S-BILL**
(Erodium cicutarium)

(from 236)

This plant resembles the well-known herb-robert (see 239) apart from its pointed petals and the arrangement of its leaves. These are divided into many leaflets growing in opposite pairs, and the leaflets themselves are similarly divided. The small pink

flowers (12–14mm) are in loose clusters of 2–5, each with an individual stalk. They develop into long, beaked fruits. Stork's-bill likes sandy ground and often grows by the sea-shore or in dry fields. Flowers June–September.

239

HERB-ROBERT
(Geranium robertianum)

(from 235)

The bright pink flowers have rounded petals and grow singly or in loose clusters. The leaves are composed of 3 or 5 leaflets and the leaflets are deeply divided. Some stems may be upright but they are inclined to straggle, so that a plant covers a wide area. The stem, stalks and leaves turn noticeably red as summer progresses. Often grows on walls or in stony places, also in woodland. Flowers May–September.

240   Are the leaves lobed?

(from 226)

Answer 'Yes' if there are several deep indentations in the margins of each leaf. These are known as lobes. Answer 'No' if the margins are not indented, though they may be toothed.

Yes 241   No 242

Unlobed

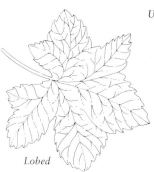

Lobed

241 COMMON MALLOW
(Malva sylvestris)

(from 240)

The pink heart-shaped petals are quite narrow at their bases, so that each is distinct from its neighbour. The flowers ($2\frac{1}{2}$–4cm) grow in small clusters of 2–5 blooms, each with its individual stalk. The clusters rise from the points where the leaf-stalks join the stem. Sometimes the plant is hairy but this is variable. Mallows prefer dry ground and grow in open country on arable ground or wasteland. They flower June–September.

242 Are the leaves fleshy?

(from 240)

Answer 'Yes' if the toothed leaves are noticeably thick and fleshy. Otherwise answer 'No'.

Yes 243   No 244

243 ORPINE
(Sedum telephium)

(from 242)

Orpine usually has several upright, unbranched stems growing quite close together. They are often tinged with red; the toothed, unstalked leaves are arranged alternately along them. The rose-red flowers (9–12mm) are in close, rounded clusters at the end of the stems. It is almost always found in woods and hedgerows. Flowers July–September.

244 Are the leaves stalkless?

(from 242)

Answer 'Yes' if the leaves have no stalks, or extremely short ones. Answer 'No' if leaf stalks are definitely present.

Yes 245   No 246

245 REDSHANK
(Polygonum persicaria)

(from 244)

The tiny pink flowers grow in very compact spikes. The largest spike is at the head of the stem, with the others, if any, from stalks branching to each side of it. The leaves are narrow and taper to a point; they often have black blotches on them. Redshank is a weed of cultivated ground or grassland. Usually prefers a damp site. Flowers June–October.

246 Is the plant a climber?

(from 244)

Answer 'Yes' if it grows by twining itself around other vegetation. Otherwise answer 'No'.

Yes 125   No 247

247 AMPHIBIOUS BISTORT
(Polygonum amphibium)

(from 246)

This plant occurs in two different forms. Either it grows in water, with its roots completely submerged and its leaves floating on the water, or on damp ground, usually near a river, when its stem is mostly procumbent, lying along the ground and putting out roots at intervals. Otherwise it is extremely like redshank (see 245) apart from its stalked leaves. Flowers July–September.

land form

water form

Is it broad-leaved?

(from 216)

Answer 'Yes' if at least some of the leaves are less than twice as long as they are broad. Answer 'No' if all of them are narrow.

Yes 249   No 250

Narrow

Broad-leaved

| 249 |

BROAD-LEAVED HELLEBORINE
(from 248) *(Epipactis helleborine)*

This orchid is distinguished by the relatively broad leaves growing towards the base of its erect stem. The flowers, which are greenish red, are in a long loose spike, all to one side of the stem. Broad-leaved helleborine may reach a height of 80cm. It grows in woods or hedgerows. Flowers July–October.

| 250 |
Does each flower have a long, narrow spur?
(from 248)

The remaining three species covered are all orchids, whose flowers are in quite a dense spike at the top of a single, erect stem. Examine a flower carefully and answer 'Yes' if there is a narrow spur, 11–13mm in length, pointing downwards and backwards from its base. Answer 'No' if the spur is shorter and more rounded.

Yes 251   No 252

Long narrow spur

Spur shorter and rounder

251 FRAGRANT ORCHID
(Gymnadenia conopsea)

(from 250)

As its name indicates, this orchid is sweet-smelling, especially in the evening. Like other orchids, it is hairless and has narrow, pointed leaves embracing the stem, especially towards its base. The flowers vary from quite pale pink to magenta. This plant usually grows on dry grassland, occasionally in marshes. Flowers June–July.

252 Do the flowers have long green bracts?

(from 250)

A bract looks exactly like a small, pointed leaf. Answer 'Yes' if, along the whole length of the flowering spike, there are many prominent green bracts intermingled with the blooms. Answer 'No' if the spikes of flowers have inconspicuous bracts the same colour as the stem.

Yes 253   No 254

253 COMMON SPOTTED ORCHID
(Dactylorhiza fuchsii)

(from 252)

The flowers of common spotted orchid are usually pink, but they may be pinkish-white or even pure white. The leaves growing at the base of the plant are less narrow than those higher up the stem, which they embrace. In both cases they may have black spots (as in the illustration) but these are sometimes absent. Usually found in open woods and grassland. Flowers June–August.

254

(from 252)

EARLY PURPLE ORCHID
(Orchis mascula)

This is the first orchid to be seen in bloom in springtime. The flowers are usually bright purple, but may be much lighter coloured. The leaves are quite similar to those of the common spotted orchid (see 253) and, again, may or may not have black spots. The single stems are hairless and erect. Usually found in open woods or scrub, occasionally in grassland. Flowers April–June.

255

(from 192)

Are the flowers regular?

Answer 'Yes' if all the petals of each flower are equal in size and the same shape. Otherwise answer 'No'.

Yes |256| No |275|

256

(from 255)

Are the leaves composite?

Answer 'Yes' if each leaf is composed of several separate leaflets; 'No' if the leaves are each single and independent.

Yes |257| No |260|

257

(from 256)

Are the leaflets opposite?

Answer 'Yes' if the leaflets are in opposite pairs along the leaf stalk. Answer 'No' if all or most of the leaves are composed of 3 leaflets, which grow in opposite pairs along the stem.

Yes |258| No |259|

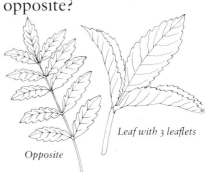

Leaf with 3 leaflets

Opposite

COMMON VALERIAN
(Valeriana officinalis)

(from 257)

Valerian grows erect with a single stem, usually unbranched. Its compound leaves are composed of small leaflets, which grow in opposite pairs and may or may not be toothed. The leaves at the base of the plant have noticeable stalks but these get progressively shorter. The small pink flowers (5mm) grow in tight clusters. Valerian prefers a damp site and grows in grassland or wasteland. Flowers June–August.

HEMP-AGRIMONY
(Eupatorium cannabinum)

(from 257)

This tall plant (30–170cm) usually grows with several upright stems, which are sometimes tinged with pink. Each flowerhead is composed of 5–6 very small tubular florets, and several flowerheads are grouped together to form loose clusters. The stem leaves are divided into 3 toothed leaflets, which are almost stalkless and arranged in opposite pairs. Hemp-agrimony grows on damp ground and flowers July–September.

| 260 |
(from 256)

How many petals has each flower?

Count the number of petals in each flower and choose your answer accordingly.

4 261
5 266
6 274

261 Are the flowers bell-shaped?

(from 260)

Answer 'Yes' if the petals of each flower are fused together in the shape of a bell or tube, so that no individual petals can be clearly distinguished. Otherwise answer 'No'.

Yes 262   No 263

Bell-shaped

262 BELL HEATHER
(Erica cinerea)
(from 261) CROSS-LEAVED HEATH
(Erica tetralix)

These two heathers are distinguished from the third species most commonly seen (see 264) by their bell-shaped flowers. The two species are rather similar and it is best to take them together. The main difference is that the leaves of the bell heather are in whorls of 3 around their stems, whilst those of the cross-leaved heath are in whorls of 4. Also the latter's flowers tend to be purple, whilst those of the bell heather are more of a rose-pink. Both species grow on acid ground, usually moorland or mountain. Flowers June–September.

Bell heather

Cross-leaved heath

263 Is the stem woody?

(from 261)

Answer 'Yes' if the plant is a heather, with a thick bushy growth and a tough woody stem. Otherwise answer 'No'.

Yes 264   No 265

264   HEATHER
(Calluna vulgaris)
(from 263)

This heather, also known as ling, should be distinguished from the two species with bell-shaped flowers (see 262). The flowers, which grow in close spikes at the end of woody stems, have 4 clearly defined petals when fully opened. The tiny leaves (1–2mm) are stalkless and arranged in opposite pairs, not whorled. The whole plant is often bushy. Heather grows on acid ground, almost always mountain or moorland. Flowers July–September.

265   GREAT WILLOWHERB
(Epilobium hirsutum)
BROAD-LEAVED WILLOWHERB
(Epilobium montanum)
(from 263)

Many species of willowherb, all rather similar, are found in the British Isles, but only the three commonest are covered in this book. One of these has alternate leaves and slightly irregular flowers and is therefore not included in this section (see 225). The two remaining species are taken together here to assist identification.

Both are erect plants with flowers in loose clusters on individual stems. The main difference is that the flowers of great willowherb (15–23mm) are larger and more purple than those of broad-leaved willowherb (6–9mm). The leaves in both cases are toothed, but broad-leaved willowherb's have very

Great willowherb

definite stalks, whilst great willowherb's are almost or completely stalkless. A final important distinction is that great willowherb is almost always found in damp places, often by a river, whilst broad-leaved willowherb prefers shady hedgerows, gardens and wasteland. Both flower June–August.

Broad-leaved willowherb

266 What size are the flowers?

(from 260)

Measure the diameter of an average flower and choose your answer accordingly.

Up to 5mm 267
10–15mm 268
Over 18mm 271

267 SAND SPURREY
(*Spergularia rubra*)

(from 266)

This little plant has many sprawling stems and seldom stands erect. Its flowers are very small and so are its leaves. The flowers (3–5mm) are pink and star-like with undivided petals and prominent green sepals; they grow singly on individual stalks.

The leaves are very narrow and sharp pointed, growing in whorls around the stems. Sand spurrey likes lime-free soil and is found growing in sandy ground especially in grassland and wasteland. Flowers May–September.

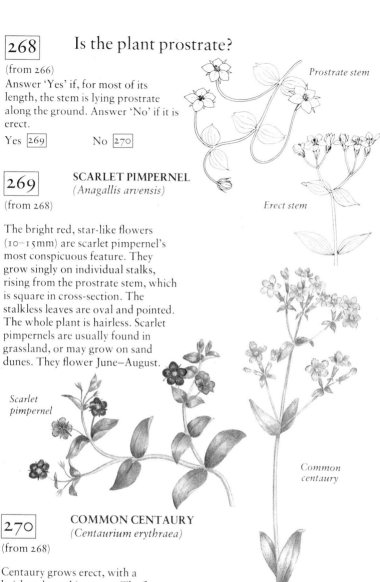

268   Is the plant prostrate?

(from 266)

Answer 'Yes' if, for most of its
length, the stem is lying prostrate
along the ground. Answer 'No' if it is
erect.

Yes 269   No 270

Prostrate stem

269   SCARLET PIMPERNEL
         (Anagallis arvensis)

(from 268)

Erect stem

The bright red, star-like flowers
(10–15mm) are scarlet pimpernel's
most conspicuous feature. They
grow singly on individual stalks,
rising from the prostrate stem, which
is square in cross-section. The
stalkless leaves are oval and pointed.
The whole plant is hairless. Scarlet
pimpernels are usually found in
grassland, or may grow on sand
dunes. They flower June–August.

*Scarlet
pimpernel*

*Common
centaury*

270   COMMON CENTAURY
         (Centaurium erythraea)

(from 268)

Centaury grows erect, with a
hairless, branching stem. The flowers
(10–15mm) are in quite loose clusters
without noticeable stalks. The paired
leaves, which are stalkless, may be
either rounded or pointed. This plant
is found in dry grassland or on sand
dunes. Flowers June–October.

Are the leaves hairless?

| 271 |

(from 266)
Answer 'Yes' if the leaves, though they may be rough to the touch, are completely without hairs. Answer 'No' if they are hairy.

Yes | 272 | No | 273 |

| 272 | **RAGGED-ROBIN**
(Lychnis flos-cuculi)

(from 271)

Each of the rose-red petals is extremely deeply divided into four very narrow segments. The flowers grow in a very loose cluster, sometimes singly, each with its own stalk. The paired leaves are narrow and pointed; the lower ones are stalked. Ragged-robin prefers damp ground and is usually found in water meadows and moist woodland. Flowers May–August.

Ragged-robin

| 273 | **RED CAMPION**
(Silene dioica)

(from 271)

The petals are heart-shaped. At the base of each flower (18–25mm) there is a hairy brown tube. The flowers grow in small, loose clusters at the end of erect stems. The upper leaves, but not the lower ones, are stalkless. Usually found in woodland edges and hedgerows. Flowers May–June.

Red campion

| 274 | **PURPLE LOOSESTRIFE**
(Lythrum salicaria)

(from 260)

This plant is very conspicuous, with its tall erect stem and the very long spike of stalkless, purple flowers

(10–15mm) growing in whorls around it. The stem is square and hairless. There are short, pointed bracts, looking like small leaves, below each whorl of flowers. The leaves grow in opposite pairs or in whorls of 3; they are untoothed, narrow and stalkless. Purple loose-strife almost always grows in damp places, often close to water. Flowers June–August.

Purple loosestrife

275 Is the plant a climber?

(from 255)

Answer 'Yes' if it grows by twining itself around other vegetation. Answer 'No' if the stem is upright and self-supporting.

Yes 70   No 276

276 Are the leaves hairless?

(from 275)

Answer 'Yes' if the leaves are completely without hairs. Answer 'No' if they are noticeably downy.

Yes 277   No 278

277   COMMON FIGWORT
(*Scrophularia nodosa*)

(from 276)

The small flowers of the figwort are not at all conspicuous. Partly reddish-brown and partly green, they grow in open clusters from the branching head of the stem. The leaves are pointed and toothed. Figwort likes damp ground and grows in moist woodland or hedgerows. Flowers June–September.

Common figwort

Do the flowers grow in separate whorls?

(from 276)

Answer 'Yes' if the flowers grow in separate whorls around the stem. Answer 'No' if all the whorls grow together in a loose spike at the top of the stem.

Yes 279   No 280

Separate whorls

Whorls in loose spike

279 **RED DEAD-NETTLE**
(Lamium purpureum)

(from 278)

This plant seldom has many flowers. They grow in little whorls around the stem, with a pair of leaves underneath each whorl. The leaves, which are stalked and toothed, are heart-shaped or may be rounded. They do not sting. The red dead-nettle grows more or less erect but does not exceed 30cm in height. It grows on arable land as well as on wasteground and in hedgerows. Flowers March–October.

280 **COMMON HEMP-NETTLE**
(Galeopsis tetrahit)
HEDGE WOUNDWORT
(Stachys sylvatica)

(from 278)

These 2 species are quite similar and it is convenient to take them together. In both cases, the purple flowers grow in whorls forming a

Red dead-nettle

loose spike at the end of the stem, with a small pair of leaves below each whorl. The leaves of hedge woundwort are heart-shaped and generally have longer stalks. The best distinguishing feature is that hemp-nettle's stem is noticeably swollen beneath each point where the leaf-stalks joins it, whereas woundwort's is straight-sided. In both cases, the stems are noticeably hairy. Woundwort has a preference for shady places in woods and hedgerows; hemp-nettle is also found on arable land. Both flower July–September.

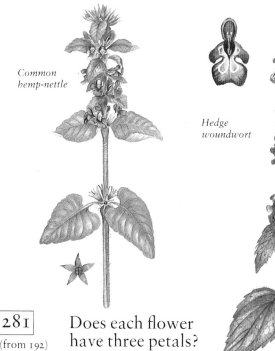

Common hemp-nettle

Hedge woundwort

281	Does each flower

(from 192) have three petals?

This question needs no elaboration.

Yes 282   No 287

282	Are the leaves very long and narrow?

(from 281)

Answer 'Yes' if the leaves are extremely narrow, many times longer than they are broad, and much the same breadth for all their length. Otherwise answer 'No'.   Yes 283   No 284

283
(from 282)

FLOWERING-RUSH
(Butomus umbellatus)

This waterside plant is at once recognized by its handsome pink flowers, which grow in a cluster, each with its own stalk, at the end of the unbranched stems. The narrow leaves have triangular cross-sections and usually grow taller than the stems, perhaps to 100cm. Always found in or beside water. Flowers June–August.

284
(from 282)

Are the leaves shaped like arrowheads?

Answer 'Yes' if the plant has leaves of an unusual shape, resembling arrowheads. Answer 'No' if they are oval with pointed tips.

Yes 285   No 286

Arrowhead-like leaf

Oval pointed leaf

285
(from 284 and 89)

ARROWHEAD
(Sagittaria sagittifolia)

The flowers (3cm) are white with purple centres. They grow in whorls of 3–5, forming a loose spike at the end of each flowering stem. The hairless leaves have very long stalks.

Arrowhead always grows in water. Some leaves are submerged below the surface; these are very long and narrow but you probably will not see them. Flowers July–August.

WATER-PLANTAIN
(Alisma plantago-aquatica)

(from 284)

The flowers (10mm) may be pale pink or white. They grow on quite long stalks in whorled clusters from branches at the end of the stems. The leaves have long stalks and are oval with pointed tips. Always found growing in or near water. Flowers June–August.

287 Is the plant growing in or beside water?

(from 281)

Answer 'Yes' if at least the root of the plant is growing in water, or if it is close beside a river or lake, or in a marsh or swamp. Answer 'No' if it is growing on dry land.

Yes 288   No 289

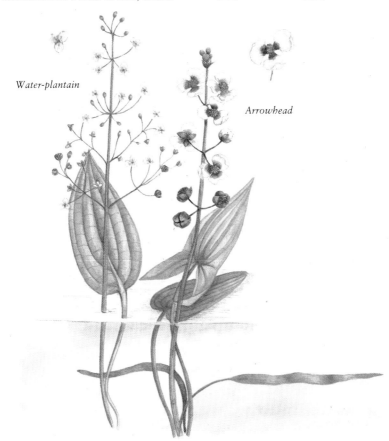

Water-plantain

Arrowhead

| 288 |

(from 287)

BOGBEAN
(Menyanthes trifoliata)

This handsome water plant has distinctive flowers and leaves. The flowers (15mm) are pink and white; their 5 petals form a star and they are covered with cottony hairs. They grow in a loose cluster at the end of a long stem. The leaves are each divided into 3 large oval leaflets at the ends of separate stalks, rising up from the roots. Bogbean always grows in or beside water, or on very wet bogland. Flowers May–July.

| 289 |

(from 287)

Does each plant have many crowded flowerheads?

Answer 'Yes' if each stout, straight stem is topped with a close-growing mass of crowded rounded flowerheads, each comprising many flowers. Answer 'No' if each stem has a single flowerhead.

Yes 290   No 291

Many crowded flowerheads   Single flowerhead

290 BUTTERBUR
(Petasites hybridus)

(from 289
and 188)

The very small pinkish flowers grow
close together in flowerheads, which
are grouped to form clusters at the
end of short, erect stems. The flowers
come out just before the leaves,
which are heart-shaped or kidney-
shaped, with prominent teeth and
stalks. Butterbur grows in damp
places, in meadows, open woodland
or on roadsides. Flowers March–
May.

291 THRIFT
(Armeria maritima)

(from 289)

The small flowers (8mm) grow in
dense rounded clusters, with a single
cluster at the end of each leafless
stem. The long narrow leaves, which
may or may not be hairy, are in
bluish-green tufts at the bases of the
stems. Thrift is usually found by the
seaside, but also grows on
mountains, salt marshes and even in
meadows. Flowers April–October.

292 Are the flowers in dense rounded flowerheads?

(from 1)

Answer 'Yes' if numerous very small
flowers are packed close together to
form a dense rounded flowerhead.
Otherwise answer 'No'.

Yes 293   No 298

293   Are the leaves prickly?

(from 292)

This question needs no elaboration.

Yes 294   No 295

294   **SEA HOLLY**
      (Eryngium maritimum)

(from 293)

Many very small flowers (8mm) are crowded together to form the unmistakable rounded flowerheads of sea holly. At the base of each flowerhead grows a circle of spiny bracts, looking like small leaves. The true leaves are stalkless, except those at the base. The whole plant is hairless. Sea holly always grows by the coast, usually in sand or shingle. Flowers July–August.

295   Are all the flowers much the same size?

(from 293)

Answer 'Yes' if all the little flowers composing each flowerhead are more or less the same size. Answer 'No' if those at the rim of each flowerhead are noticeably larger than those at the centre.

Yes 296   No 297

Outer flowers larger   *All flowers much the same size*

296   **DEVIL'S-BIT SCABIOUS**
      (Succisa pratensis)

(from 295)

The flowerheads (15–25mm) are smaller than those of field scabious (see 297) but the same shape and colour. They grow at the end of long delicate stems, which are usually branched. The narrow, pointed leaves grow in opposite pairs and may be slightly hairy. Usually found in grassland or damp woodland. Flowers June–October.

FIELD SCABIOUS
(Knautia arvensis)

Very similar to devil's-bit scabious
(see 296) but with larger flowerheads
(3–4cm) and deeply divided leaves.
This erect plant may reach a height
of 100cm. It has hairy leaves and
stems, which sometimes become
bristly. Field scabious usually grows
in grassland and hedgerows. Flowers
July–September.

Field scabious

Devil's-bit scabious

298 Are the flowers regular?

(from 292)

Answer 'Yes' if all the petals of each flower are more or less equal in size and the same shape. Answer 'No' if the flowers are so irregular that they can only be divided in 2 equal halves in one direction. (Note that the tiny flowers of the mints appear regular until examined closely with a magnifying glass, but their irregularity is so slight that they should be classed as regular.)

Yes 299   No 322

299 Does the plant smell of mint?

(from 298)

Crush a leaf between finger and thumb and smell it. Answer 'Yes' if it has a strong smell of mint; otherwise answer 'No'.

Yes 319   No 300

300 Are the flowers bell-shaped?

(from 299)

Answer 'Yes' if the flowers are shaped more or less like a bell: the petals are fused together or so closely overlapping that they cannot easily be distinguished. Answer 'No' if each petal is clearly distinct down to its base.

Yes 301   No 305

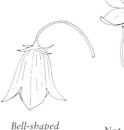

Bell-shaped   *Not bell-shaped*

301 Are the leaves basal only?

(from 300)

Answer 'Yes' if the leaves grow only at the base of the plant, so that the flowering stems are leafless. Answer 'No' if leaves also grow from the stems.

Yes 302   No 303

302 | BLUEBELL
(Hyacinthoides non-scripta)

(from 301)

The bluebell (known in Scotland as
the hyacinth) is one of the best
known and most welcome flowers,
carpeting the woodland floor with its
bright blue, sweet-scented blossoms
in early spring. The flowers dangle in
a loose cluster, all facing the same
way, at the top of the unbranched
stem. The leaves are long and very
narrow. The whole plant is hairless.
Usually found in deciduous
woodland, also in hedgerows and
grassland. Flowers April–June.

303 | Is the plant bristly?

(from 301)

Answer 'Yes' if the plant is covered
in short, stiff, bristly hairs.
Otherwise answer 'No'.

Yes | 114 | No | 304 |

304 | HAREBELL
(Campanula rotundifolia)

(from 303)

The harebell (known in Scotland as
the bluebell) is perhaps the most bell-
like of all flowers. The rim of each
blossom is edged with 5 pointed
lobes. The flowers grow singly, at
intervals along the stem, from short,
delicate stalks. The stem leaves are
alternate, quite short and very
narrow. There are also small round
leaves at the base of the plant.
Harebells grow on grassland and
heathland. Flowers July–September.

Basal leaves

305 How many petals has each flower?

(from 300)
Count the number of petals in each
flower and choose your answer
accordingly.

4 306
5 312
Over 6 317

306 How big are the flowers?

(from 305)
Measure the diameter of an average-
sized flower and choose your answer
accordingly.

3mm 307
More than 10mm 308

307 FIELD MADDER
(Sherardia arvensis)

(from 306)

The tiny lilac flowers (2–3mm),
which have long petal tubes at their
bases, grow in close clusters at the
very ends of the stems. The stems are
4-sided and most of them are
prostrate (lying along the ground).
The pointed leaves grow in whorls of
4–6 and have slightly prickly edges.
Field madder grows on farmland or
wasteland. Flowers May–October.

308 Are the leaves bristly?

(from 306)
Answer 'Yes' if the leaves are covered
in short, stiff, bristly hairs.
Otherwise answer 'No'.

Yes 117   No 309

309 Are the leaves compound?

(from 308)
Answer 'Yes' if the lower leaves bear
opposite pairs of leaflets. Answer
'No' if the leaves are simple.

Yes 310   No 311

310 CUCKOO FLOWER
(Cardamine pratensis)

(from 309
and 116)

The flowers (12–18mm) range in
colour from lilac to rose-pink to
white, but those on the same plant
are always much the same. They are
grouped in quite small clusters at the
end of each stem. The leaves are
divided into 3–7 rounded leaflets,
except the upper ones, which are
long and narrow. The whole plant is
hairless. Cuckoo flower prefers a
damp site and often grows by rivers,
or in damp meadows or woodland.
Flowers April–June.

311 FIELD GENTIAN
(Gentianella campestris)

(from 309)

The 4 petals are joined at their bases
to form a tube, which is partly
hidden by 4 conspicuous sepals. The
flowers (15mm) are in quite compact
small clusters at the end of the stem
or its branches. The hairless,
stalkless leaves are oval and pointed.
Field gentians grow in grassland or
on sand dunes. Rare in southern
England. Flowers July–October.

312 Is the plant a climber?

(from 305)

Answer 'Yes' if it grows by twining
itself around other vegetation.
Answer 'No' if the stem is upright
and self-supporting.

Yes 313   No 314

313
BITTERSWEET
(Solanum dulcamara)

(from 312)

The strongly contrasting colours of the flowers – bluish-purple petals with bright yellow anthers in the centre – make bittersweet easy to recognize. The flowers grow in little clusters from quite long stalks as the plant climbs and clambers over surrounding vegetation to a height of 200cm. The leaves are oval and pointed. Bittersweet, also known as woody nightshade, is usually found in woodland and hedgerows, but also has a liking for beaches and sand dunes. Flowers June–September.

314
Are the leaves broad?

(from 312)
Answer 'Yes' if the leaves are almost rounded in outline while at the same time deeply lobed. Answer 'No' if they are short, narrow and unlobed.

Yes 315   No 316

315
MEADOW CRANE'S-BILL
(Geranium pratense)

(from 314)

The large, sky-blue flowers (15–18mm) of meadow crane's-bill are very easy to recognize. They grow singly on quite short stalks towards the ends of the stems. The deeply divided leaves are noticeably hairy; those at the base of the plant are stalked. Usually grows in meadows or other grassland. Flowers June–September.

316 | FIELD FORGET-ME-NOT
(Myosotis arvensis)
(from 314)

The little pale blue flowers (5mm)
with yellow centres are very
noticeable. They grow in loose spikes
at the ends of the branched stems.
The whole plant is hairy and grows
fairly erect. The leaves are small,
undivided and stalkless. Found in dry
grassland, roadsides and hedges.
Flowers April–September.

(Note that there are several other
species of forget-me-not, all rather
similar, in particular the water
forget-me-not *(Myosotis
scorpioides)*, which has larger
flowers and grows in damp places;
but these are not covered in this book.)

317 | Is the plant in fresh water?

(from 305)
Answer 'Yes' if it is growing almost
submerged in fresh water. Answer
'No' if it is not far from the sea or by
an estuary.

Yes 90   No 318

318 | SEA ASTER
(Aster tripolium)
(from 317)

The decorative mauve flowers with
yellow centres (8–20mm) make this
seem like a garden flower. They grow
in loose clusters on individual stalks
at the ends of the flowering stems.
The hairless, fleshy leaves are narrow
and pointed. As its name indicates,
this plant is almost always found by
the seaside. Flowers July–October.

319
(from 299)

Does each stem end in a flowerhead?

Answer 'Yes' if the largest or only flowerhead grows at the very end of the stem. Answer 'No' if the flowers are in whorls around the stem, with none growing at its tip.

Yes 320   No 321

Flowerhead
at end of stem   Flowers in whorls

320
(from 319)

WATER MINT
(Mentha aquatica)

Water mint almost always grows in water, or in wet ground close to water. In addition to the main dense flowerhead at the end of its square stem, there may be flowers in smaller whorls around it, with a pair of leaves below each whorl. The plant is aromatic: its leaves, which are bluntly toothed, have a pleasant minty smell when crushed. Flowers July–October.

321
(from 319)

CORN MINT
(Mentha arvensis)

Corn mint bears a strong family likeness to water mint (see 320) with its square stem, downy leaves and small lilac flowers, but the flowers are in a series of whorls along the stem, with a pair of leaves under each whorl, and there is no flowerhead at the end of·the stem. The leaves of the corn mint give off a faint minty smell when crushed. The plant likes damp ground, but not as wet as water mint. Found as a weed in arable ground or in damp woods and meadows. Flowers May–October.

Corn
mint

Water
mint

322 How do the leaves grow?

(from 298)

Leaves are described as being alternate, opposite, whorled or basal, depending on how they are arranged along their stem or stalk. The drawings will help you to decide.

Alternate leaves grow singly, on alternating sides of the stem, while opposite leaves are in pairs. Choose 'Basal only' if all the leaves grow at the very base of the plant.

Alternate 323
Opposite 334
Basal only 341

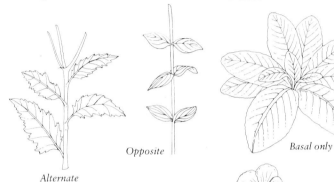

Opposite

Basal only

Alternate

323 Do the flowers grow singly?

(from 322)

Answer 'Yes' if each flower is solitary, with its own stalk to itself. Answer 'No' if several or many flowers grow close together; the flower-stalks, if any, are very short.

Yes 324   No 329

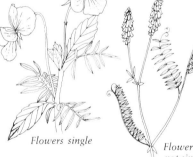

Flowers single

Flower not single

324 Are the leaves heart-shaped?

(from 323)

Answer 'Yes' if the leaves are rounded, but have indentations and come to a point so that they are more or less heart-shaped. Otherwise answer 'No'.

Yes 325   No 326

325 COMMON DOG VIOLET
(Viola riviniana)

(from 324)

Of the two best-known violets, sweet violet has all its leaves at the base of the plant and is therefore considered separately (see 341). Dog violet is scentless, unlike sweet violet, and has rather larger flowers (up to 25mm). Its hairless leaves grow from delicate stalks, either from the base of the plant or along the stems. Dog violet grows on woodland banks, in woods or shady grassland. Flowers April–June.

326 Does the plant stand erect?

(from 324)

Answer 'Yes' if its stem is strong enough to stand upright. Answer 'No' if the whole plant is prostrate, crawling low over the ground.

Yes 327 No 328

Prostrate stem

327 WILD PANSY
(Viola tricolor)

(from 57 and 326)

The flowers of wild pansy are variable in colour: they may be violet, yellow, or a combination of both. They grow singly on a delicate stalk from the fairly erect, leafy stem. There are deeply divided leaf-like stipules at the bases of the flower-stalks. Pansies grow on arable ground, wasteland or dry grassland. Flowers April–September.

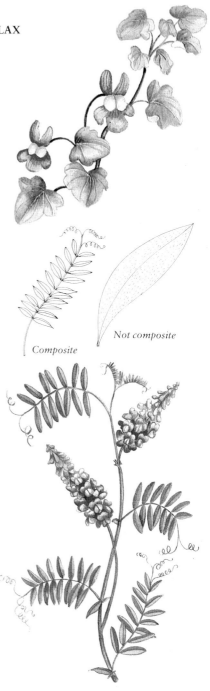

328 IVY-LEAVED TOADFLAX
(Cymbalaria muralis)

(from 326)

This plant is distinctive because it almost always grows on walls or stone steps, though it may also thrive on rocks or stony ground. The very small leaves are indeed ivy-shaped, with conspicuous pointed lobes. The flowers, too, are very small (5–10mm) and grow on short, delicate stalks. However, a single plant may cover a considerable area. Flowers May–September.

329 Are the leaves composite?

(from 323)

Answer 'Yes' if each leaf is composed of several separate leaflets. Answer 'No' if the leaves, though they may be deeply divided, are each single and independent.

Yes 330   No 331

Not composite

Composite

330 TUFTED VETCH
(Vicia cracca)

(from 329)

This is much the bluest of the common vetches and grows to the greatest size. Using its twisty tendrils, it may climb and clamber for up to 200cm over surrounding vegetation. The flowers are in long clusters of up to 40 blooms, all facing more or less the same way. Each leaf is divided into 8–12 pairs of opposite leaflets, and grows on a short stalk from the weak, twining stem. The whole plant is slightly hairy. Tufted vetch grows in hedgerows, scrubland and open woodland. Flowers June–August.

331

(from 329)
Measure the diameter of an average
flower and choose your answer
accordingly.

Over 10mm [332]
Under 10mm [333]

332   **VIPER'S-BUGLOSS**
    (Echium vulgare)

(from 331)

The bright blue flowers (10–20mm)
are extremely conspicuous. They
grow in a loose spike and have 5
irregular petals, fused together to
form a tube. The plant grows erect
and is covered in pale bristly hairs.
The leaves are narrow and very
pointed. Viper's-bugloss always
grows on dry ground and prefers
grassland; also found on cliffs and
sand dunes. Flowers June–
September.

333   **COMMON MILKWORT**
    (Polygala vulgaris)

(from 331)

This little plant has very small, bright
blue flowers (6–8mm), arranged in
long clusters at the ends of its
branched stems. The leaves are also
very small; they are narrow, pointed
and without teeth or stalks. Usually
found in grassland. Flowers May–
June.

334 Do the flowers have 4 distinct petals?

(from 322)

Answer 'Yes' if each flower has 4 distinct petals, all nearly (but not quite) the same size. Answer 'No' if the flowers are much more irregular, with or without a single upper lip and with a 3-lobed lower lip.

Yes 335   No 336

4 distinct petals   *3-lobed lower lip*

335 GERMANDER SPEEDWELL
(Veronica chamaedrys)
BROOKLIME
(Veronica beccabunga)

(from 334)

These two related species are quite similar and it is best to take them together. In both cases the upper petal is slightly larger, the lower slightly smaller than the 2 others. Speedwell's flowers (10mm) are somewhat bigger than brooklime's (5–8mm) and a rather paler blue. Moreover the latter is always hairless, while the leaves and stems of the former are noticeably hairy. Brooklime, which flowers May–September, prefers a damp site, usually near water; germander speedwell (March–July) grows in dry grassland, woods and hedgerows.

336 Is much of the stem creeping?

(from 334)

Answer 'Yes' if much of the stem is lying prostrate along the ground, rising from it to bear the leaves and flowers. Answer 'No' if the whole plant stands erect.

Yes 337   No 338

Germander speedwell

Brooklime

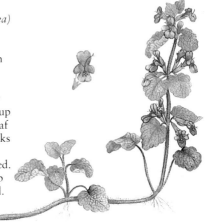

337

(from 336)

GROUND-IVY
(Glechoma hederacea)

Ground-ivy is a creeping plant with rooting stems, rising at their extremities to bear leaves and flowers. The whole plant is slightly hairy. The mauve or pink flowers, up to 2cm long, grow in pairs in the leaf axils (the points where the leaf-stalks join the stems). The long-stalked leaves are rounded or kidney-shaped. Ground-ivy usually grows on damp ground in woods and on wasteland. Flowers March–May.

338 Is the flower 2-lipped?

(from 336)

Answer 'Yes' if the flower has a hooded upper lip and a 3-lobed lower lip. Answer 'No' if the upper lip is missing.

Selfheal

Yes [339]   No [340]

Hooded upper lip   *Upper lip absent*

Bugle

339

(from 338)

SELFHEAL
(Prunella vulgaris)

Selfheal bears a superficial resemblance to bugle (see 340); but all or almost all the flowers, which are lighter and more purplish in colour, grow in a single cluster above the top pair of leaves. The leaf-stalks are longest towards the base of the plant; the leaves are oval, pointed and untoothed. Self heal grows in grassland and woods. Flowers June–September.

340 BUGLE
(Ajuga reptans)
(from 338)

Bugle's blue flowers are in diminishing whorls around its erect stem, with a small pair of leaves below each whorl. The number of whorls is very variable, as is the plant's height, which is usually less than 10cm but may reach 30cm or more. Bugle is found in damp meadows, woodland or hedgerows. Flowers April–June.

341 SWEET VIOLET
(Viola odorata)
(from 322)

Sweet violet and dog violet (see 325) are the two members of this much-loved family most commonly seen in Britain. They are most easily told apart by the sweet violet's smell, and its heart-shaped leaves which all rise from the base of the plant, not alternately along the stems. Each delicate flower-stalk bears a single flower. Sweet violet grows in woodlands and hedgerows. Flowers March–May.

342 Is the plant growing in water?
(from 1)

Answer 'Yes' if the lower part of the stem, or all the stem, is submerged in water. Answer 'No' if the plant is growing on dry land, or if only the roots are submerged.

Yes 343   No 350

343 Are the leaves very long and narrow?
(from 342)

Answer 'Yes' if all the leaves grow erect and are long and narrow, like those of a reed or iris.

Otherwise answer 'No'.

Yes 344   No 347

(from 343)
Answer 'Yes' if the very small flowers grow in a dense, erect spike, which rises vertically above the water. Otherwise answer 'No'.

Yes | 345 | No | 346 |

| 345 | **REEDMACE**
            (Typha latifolia)
(from 344)

Reedmace, generally though wrongly known as bulrush, is easily recognizable with its two heads of densely-packed flowers, one above the other on every stem. The lower of these, which is female, forms a regular cylindrical shape with rounded ends. The male flowers in the upper flowerhead are in a smaller, looser spike. Later in the year, the male flowers fall, leaving the females to develop into seed while still retaining their shape. The leaves are quite narrow and grow alternately along the stems. This species is always found in water or on very swampy ground. Flowers June–July.

Reedmace

Branched bur-reed

| 346 | **BRANCHED BUR-REED**
            (Sparganium erectum)
(from 344)

The tiny flowers grow in rounded flowerheads at the ends of the branched stems, which also bear leaves. The smaller flowerheads at the top of the stem are male, the larger ones below them are female. The main leaves grow from the base of the plant, which is normally submerged in water. Flowers June–August.

347 Do the flowers grow in a dense spike?

(from 343)

Answer 'Yes' if the flowers grow in a conspicuous spike. Answer 'No' if they grow singly and are extremely hard to find.

Yes 348   No 349

Flowers in spike

348 BROAD-LEAVED PONDWEED
(Potamogeton natans)

(from 347)

The dense spikes (3–8cm long) of tiny green flowers make this plant quite easy to recognize. It has broad, leathery, pointed leaves floating on the surface of the water, as well as narrow ones below it, which may not be visible. This pondweed grows in still water or slow-moving rivers. Flowers May–September.

349 COMMON WATER-STARWORT
(Callitriche stagnalis)

(from 347)

The flowers are so tiny, without petals or sepals, that you are quite likely not to notice them. They grow in the leaf axils (the points where the leaves join the stem). The shape of the hairless leaves is variable, either strap-shaped or oval. They float on the water or are just below the surface. Mostly they are in opposite pairs but sometimes they grow in whorls. Water-starwort grows in still or slow-moving water, occasionally on wet mud beside it. Flowers May–September.

350 How do the leaves grow?

(from 342)

Leaves are described as being alternate, opposite or basal depending on how they are arranged along their stem or stalk. The drawings will help you to decide.

Alternate leaves grow singly, on alternating sides of the stem. Opposite leaves are in pairs. Choose 'basal only' if all the leaves grow at the very base of the plant.

Alternate 351
Opposite 364
Basal only 369

Alternate

Opposite

Basal only

351 Are the flowers without petals or sepals?

(from 350)

Answer 'Yes' if the little green flowers are quite without petals or sepals. They consist only of an ovary and stamens, though beneath these is a circle of leaf-like bracts, which might be mistaken for part of the flower. Answer 'No' if the plant quite clearly has petals or sepals, though they may be very small.

No petals or sepals

Yes 352   No 353

352

(from 351)

PETTY SPURGE
(Euphorbia peplus)
SUN SPURGE
(Euphorbia helioscopia)

These two spurges are similar and it is best to take them together. They are difficult species because the flowers are so tiny that you might not think they are in bloom. In sun spurge, the bracts (see 351) are yellowish and grow in whorls under the flowers. In the petty spurge they are greener and tend to be opposite.

Petty spurge

Both species are erect and hairless. Sun spurge reaches a greater height (50cm) and has stalkless leaves; petty spurge's leaves have short stalks and the plant does not exceed 30cm. Both are found on arable ground and wasteland. Petty spurge flowers April–November, sun spurge May–October.

Sun spurge

353

(from 351)

Do the flowers have 6 sepals and no petals?

Examine the flowers very carefully. Those of the dock and sorrel, which are extremely small, have 6 sepals and no petals. Three of these sepals are so tiny that you may not notice them at first. The other three are petal-like, till they fall as the seeds ripen and turn red. Answer 'Yes' if your plant is one of these. Otherwise answer 'No'.

Yes 354   No 357

354

(from 353)

Do the leaves have an acid taste?

Chew one of the leaves. Answer 'Yes' if it tastes distinctly acid or sour. Otherwise answer 'No'.

Yes 355   No 356

355

(from 354)

COMMON SORREL
(Rumex acetosa)

The leaves are long and narrow, with pointed lobes at their bases. Those towards the base have long stalks, but the upper ones are stalkless. The little green flowers, which become tinged with red, are in loose whorls around the branched stems.
Common sorrel is hairless and grows upright. As the summer goes by, the whole plant tends to turn red. It grows in grassland, woodland and on waste ground. Flowers May–June.

356 BROAD-LEAVED DOCK
(Rumex obtusifolia)

(from 354)

This unbeautiful flower is a common farmland weed and also grows on wasteland. The tiny flowers have 6 sepals and no petals; they grow in whorls. The stem is branched and tends to be tinged with red, as do the seeds when they ripen. The leaves are fairly broad, with pointed or rounded tips, and may grow to a great size – up to 25cm in length. Their undersides may be hairy. Flowers June–October.

357 How many petals has each flower?

(from 353)

Count the number of petals in each flower and choose your answer accordingly.

4 | 358
5 | 359
6 | 139

358 LADY'S-MANTLE
(Alchemilla vulgaris)

(from 357)

The tiny green flowers (3–5mm) have no true petals, but 4 petal-like, pointed sepals. They grow in small clusters at the ends of the branched stems. The toothed leaves grow mainly at the base of the plant; they are quite deeply lobed and have long stalks. Others, which are more rounded, grow alternately along the stem and are stalkless. Grows in grassland, usually meadows. Flowers ʻune–September.

359	## Is the plant a climber?

(from 357)

Answer 'Yes' if it grows by twining itself around other vegetation or clinging to it. Answer 'No' if the stem is upright and self-supporting.

Yes 360   No 363

360	## Are the flowers extremely small?

(from 359)

Answer 'Yes' if the flowers are tiny – no more than 5mm in diameter. Answer 'No' if they exceed 10mm.

Yes 361   No 362

361	**IVY** *(Hedera helix)*

(from 360)

Ivy's flowers are often extremely difficult to find because, apart from being so small, they grow only on the uppermost part of the plant, which may climb to a height of over 30m. They are in small rounded clusters, which become more conspicuous when the bright green berries develop, and later turn black. Ivy, with its woody stem and deeply lobed leaves, is well-known on trees almost everywhere. Flowers September–November.

362	**WHITE BRYONY** *(Bryonia dioica)*

(from 360 and 124)

The male flowers (12–18mm) grow on stalks in small clusters. The female flowers are smaller and very inconspicuous, till they turn to red berries. The leaves are very deeply lobed. Twining tendrils grow directly from the angled stem, enabling the plant to clamber over surrounding vegetation. Usually found in hedgerows and woodland. Flowers May–September.

363

(from 359)

FAT-HEN
(Chenopodium album)
COMMON ORACHE
(Atriplex patula)

male flower   *female flower*

These two plants are similar and it is best to take them together. The main distinction is that the orache has different male and female flowers, whilst fat-hen's flowers are all the same. In both cases, the spikes of flowers rise from the leaf axils (where the leaves join the stem). Fat-hen's stem is very often reddish. The leaves are very variable. Both plants are found on cultivated ground or wasteland. Flower July–September, the fat-hen till October.

Common orache

364

(from 350)

Does the plant grow upright?

Answer 'Yes' if it grows with an upright, self-supporting stem. Answer 'No' if most of the stems are lying along the ground, rising only towards their extremities.

Yes 365   No 368

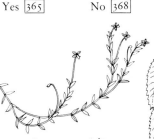

Stems not upright   *Upright stem*

Fat-hen

365

Are the flowers in hanging spikes?

(from 364)

Answer 'Yes' if the tiny flowers grow in long, hanging spikes. Answer 'No' if the spikes are upright.

Yes 366   No 367

366 COMMON NETTLE
(Urtica dioica)

(from 365)

Almost everyone knows the rightly unpopular nettle, with its pointed, stinging leaves, which grow in opposite pairs and are noticeably toothed. The tiny flowers are in dangling spikes growing in the leaf axils (the points where the leaves join the stem). Nettles grow mainly on wasteland and in woods. Flowers June–August.

Common nettle

Dog's mercury

male flowers

female flowers

367 DOG'S MERCURY
(Mercurialis perennis)

(from 365)

Plants of this species are either male or female. In both cases, the little green flowers are very inconspicuous. Both sexes have 3 regular, pointed, petal-like sepals. The male flowers have yellow stamens in the centres; they grow in long upright spikes from the leaf-axils (where the leaves join the stems). The females are smaller and even less noticeable, on 3cm stalks in groups of 1–3. The leaves are hairy, oval and pointed. Dog's mercury usually grows in woodland. Flowers February–April.

368 PROCUMBENT PEARLWORT
(Sagina procumbens)

(from 364)

This is such a small plant, with tiny flowers (4mm) and small, very narrow leaves, that it often escapes attention. The flowers normally have no true petals, but 4 pointed petal-like sepals. They grow on stalks rising from procumbent runners, which spread along the ground from a central rosette of leaves. Pearlwort usually grows on lawns, other grassy places or pathways. Flowers June–August.

369 Are the flowers arranged in a loose spike?

(from 350)

Answer 'Yes' if the orchid-like flowers are in a loose spike, all facing much the same way, along the upper half of the stem. Otherwise answer 'No'.

Yes 370

No 371

Flowers in loose spike

370 COMMON TWAYBLADE
(Listera ovata)

(from 369)

This is a member of the orchid family and has distinctive orchid-like flowers in a loose spike at the top of its single stem. It is also easily recognized by the broad, opposite leaves, which grow in a pair (never more) near the base of the stem. Twayblade is found in damp woods and grassland. It flowers June–July.

371 Are the leaves narrow?

(from 369)

Answer 'Yes' if the leaf is at least 5 times as long as it is wide. Answer 'No' if it is not more than 3 times as long as it is wide.

Yes 372   No 373

372 RIBWORT PLANTAIN
(Plantago lanceolata)

(from 371)

This is the very well-known plantain that grows everywhere in fields, lawns and other grassland. It can be confused only with the greater plantain (see 373), whose spike of tiny flowers is longer and greener. The ribwort plantain also has much narrower leaves. Flowers April–October.

373 GREATER PLANTAIN
(Plantago major)

(from 371)

The flowers are in long green spikes at the ends of stems which rise upright from the rosette of leaves at the base. The spikes are much longer, the leaves less narrow and the stems usually shorter than in the case of the better known ribwort plantain (see 372). Usually grows in fields and other grassy places. Flowers June–October.

Index and Checklist

Use the boxes to mark with an 'x' each new species as you see it. There are spare boxes at the end for you to insert other species that are not included in the book.

ENGLISH NAMES

SCIENTIFIC NAMES